D0408846

Garrick's Folly

In 1769, for the first time, a great Shakespeare Jubilee festival was held at Stratford, under the direction of David Garrick. The occasion was the dedication of the new town hall and the presentation by Garrick of a statue of Shakespeare. Immense interest, enthusiasm, and controversy were aroused by the plans, which involved not only theatrical and rhetorical festivities but fireworks, processions and a horserace.

This book describes the festival, which touched heights of success and depths of disaster, its impact on Stratford, its after effects in London, especially theatrical London, where rival managers tried to cash in on Garrick's idea and where Garrick turned the Stratford failure into resounding success at Drury Lane. The author quotes entertainingly from newspapers, memoirs, and plays, and illustrates her book with contemporary engravings and portraits.

Garrick embracing the Bust of Shakespeare

(Engraving by Valentine Greene from Thomas Gainsborough's painting commissioned by the Stratford upon Avon Corporation for their new Town Hall. The original painting was destroyed by fire in 1946.)

Garrick's Folly

THE SHAKESPEARE JUBILEE OF 1769
AT STRATFORD AND DRURY LANE

by Johanne M. Stochholm

BARNES & NOBLE INC
NEW YORK

First published in 1964
© *Johanne M. Stochholm,* 1964
Printed in Great Britain by
Richard Clay & Co Ltd
The Chaucer Press, Bungay, Suffolk

Published in the United States in 1964
by Barnes & Noble, Inc., 105 *Fifth Avenue*
New York 3

To
Frederick A. Pottle
in gratitude

Contents

I   Planning and Preparations   *page* 1

II   Description of the Jubilee   51

III Public Reactions to the Jubilee   108

IV The Jubilee on the London Stage: the
      Rival Managers   143

      Index   175

Illustrations

I. PLATES

Garrick Embracing the Bust of Shakespeare *frontispiece*
(*Engraving by Valentine Greene from Thomas Gainsborough's painting commissioned by the Stratford upon Avon Corporation for their new Town Hall. The original painting was destroyed by fire in 1946.*)

1 New Place with Guildhall and Chapel *facing page* 6
(*from R. B. Wheler's* History and Antiquities of Stratford)

2 The Mulberry Box 7
(*now in the British Museum*)

3 Commemorative Handkerchief 54
(*in the possession of the Shakespeare Birthplace Trust: believed to be unique*)

4 The Scene at the High Cross 55
(*contemporary water-colour in the possession of the Shakespeare Birthplace Trust*)

5 Garrick as Steward 62
(*Engraving by T. Saunders from the painting by Benjamin Van der Gucht*)

6 The Jubilee Medal 63

Garrick's Medallion
(*Shakespeare Birthplace Trust*)

7 Thomas King and Mrs Baddeley, in *The Clandestine Marriage* 88
(*oil painting in the possession of the Garrick Club*)

8 Dr Arne 89
(*Engraving from a drawing by Bartolozzi*)

9 Samuel Foote 118
(*oil painting in the possession of the Garrick Club*)

ix

10 The Procession at Stratford (as it should have been)   119
     (*from the* Oxford Magazine, *September and October* 1769)

11 The Rival Managers   152
     (*from the* Ladies' Magazine, *September,* 1769)

12 Title-page to *The Jubilee* or *Shakespeare's Garland*   153
     (*from* The Stratford Jubilee, *a scrapbook, British Museum*)

II. ILLUSTRATIONS IN TEXT

Shakespeare's Birthplace   *page* 2
     (*from* The Gentleman's Magazine, *July* 1679)

The Amphitheatre   13
     (*from* The Gentleman's Magazine, *September* 1769)

Ticket of Admission   36
     (*in possession of the Folger Shakespeare Library*)

The Loving Cup   60
     (*from a newspaper cutting in* The Stratford Jubilee, *a scrapbook, British Museum*)

Garrick Reciting the Ode at Stratford   70
     (*from* The Town and Country Magazine, *September* 1769)

Boswell as a Corsican Chief   99
     (*from* The London Magazine, *September,* 1769)

The Jubilee Handbill   104
     (*British Museum*)

Garrick Reciting the Ode at Drury Lane   124
     (*British Museum*)

Principal Characters in the Procession   154–5
     (*Anonymous engraving found lying loose in* John Payne Collier's *own copy of his* English Dramatic Poetry *at the Folger Shakespeare Library*)

ACKNOWLEDGEMENTS

I am most grateful to the following persons and institutions for allowing me to reproduce the illustrations mentioned: the British Museum (Frontispiece, Plates 2, 5, 8, 11, 12; illustrations on pp. 60, 99, 104, 124); the Folger Shakespeare Library (illustrations on pp. 36, 154–5); the Garrick Club (Plates 7 and 9); the Royal Shakespeare Theatre Library (Plate 10); the Shakespeare Birthplace Trust (Plates 1, 3, 4)

Preface

As a small contribution to the celebrations due in 1964 to mark the quatercentenary of Shakespeare's birth, it occurred to me that it might be appropriate to give a fairly detailed account of the first national Shakespeare Festival, the Stratford Jubilee in 1769. The circumstances that led to the planning of a Jubilee at that particular time, the preparations made for it, the misfortunes encountered during the three-day celebration, and the literary and dramatic activities aroused by it in the months immediately following seem to me sometimes pathetic, sometimes amusing, but definitely interesting.

My object has not been to prove anything new about the Jubilee, but to reconstruct it in full and authentic detail. In order to accomplish this I have drawn indiscriminately on documents already collected by others and on matter turned up by my own examination of contemporary newspapers, periodicals, pamphlets, and books, such as biographies and memoirs, etc.

I want to thank Professor Frederick A. Pottle of Yale University and Dr James G. McManaway of the Folger Shakespeare Library for encouragement and advice during the preparation of this work, and likewise to thank Ethel Ramage and Sarah T. Ramage of Sweet Briar College, Virginia; Margaret P. Boddy, Winona College, Minnesota; Donald W. Hannah and Ann Draycon of the University of Aarhus; and Michael P. Rhodes of University College, London, for valuable suggestions and some clerical assistance. I am grateful to Sweet Briar College for a faculty grant that made it possible for me to obtain needed photostats of rare materials and to Aarhus University, Denmark, for exemption from teaching duties during the spring semester of 1963.

I wish to thank the Folger Shakespeare Library for permission to quote matter from *Garrickiana I*, *Collectanea*, the Garrick manuscript *Journal of Journey to France* and Italy, Messink *Order of the Pageant in the Jubilee* (references to all of which will be found in footnotes *passim*): also Messrs. Heinemann and the McGraw Hill Book Company for the use of material in *The Private Papers of James Boswell*, 6, *Boswell in Search of a Wife* (edited by Frank Brady and Frederick A. Pottle). (My page references are to the American edition.) I also gratefully acknowledge the use I have been able to make of 'The Jubilee', the manuscript which was discovered by Professor Elizabeth P. Stein in the Huntington Library and published by her in *Three Plays by David Garrick*.

I should like to express my gratitude for efficient and courteous service received at the British Museum, the Folger Shakespeare Library, the Yale University Library, the Libraries of the Shakespeare Birthplace Trust, the Royal Shakespeare Theatre, the Shakespeare Museum, Stratford upon Avon and the Garrick Club.

Aarhus University,   JOHANNE M. STOCHHOLM
Aarhus, Denmark
September 1963

I

Planning and Preparations

It is surprising to the modern reader and theatre-goer that no large Shakespeare Festival should have been held before 1769, but it must be remembered that although some of his plays were performed during the Restoration period, they were not nearly so popular with audiences as the plays of Jonson and of Beaumont and Fletcher. It should, however, be noted that many editions of Shakespeare's plays had been published before 1769. The First Folio had been reprinted in 1632, 1663, and 1685, and in the eighteenth century a number of editions had appeared, the most important being those of Rowe (1709), Pope (1723–25), Theobald (1733–34), Warburton (1747), Johnson (1765), and Capell (1768). Dryden had given high praise to Shakespeare as a dramatist in his *Essay of Dramatic Poesy* (1668). In the early years of the eighteenth century Shakespeare's plays were coming into their own again and were more frequently performed (although often in altered versions) than those of his contemporaries. Their popularity was much increased when David Garrick, the famous actor, during his long career (1747–76) as actor and later actor-manager of Drury Lane Theatre, produced twenty-seven of the plays and acted in many of them. His efforts on behalf of his favourite author were so successful that a very real interest in Shakespeare and his plays was evident in London in 1769, the year of the Stratford Jubilee.

Before this time comparatively little interest had been taken in Stratford as Shakespeare's birthplace. Some writers, critics, and actors did occasionally visit Stratford — Garrick, for instance, had been there as a young man in 1744 — but no concerted effort had been made to draw the general public to the town. However, with the

A House in Stratford upon Avon, in which the famous Poet Shakespear was Born.

Shakespeare's Birthplace
(from *The Gentleman's Magazine*, July 1769)

growing interest in Shakespeare shown by London audiences the people of Stratford began to realize the importance of Shakespeare and of everything connected with him in the town, such as the house where he was born and his tomb and monument in the church. Unfortunately New Place, Shakespeare's big house in Stratford, had under the most peculiar circumstances been torn down by its owner in 1759. To explain this happening it is necessary to give a brief account of its history.

In 1597 Shakespeare had bought a house erected by Sir Hugh Clopton during the reign of Henry VIII, the largest and best house in town, originally known as the Great House, but at a later date renamed New Place. To this he retired in 1613 when he left the London stage. In the garden near the house he planted with his own hand a mulberry tree, at a time (1609) when King James was urging the English to plant such trees in the hope of developing a silk industry. Here at New Place he died in 1616. The property was left in his will to his daughter, Mrs Susannah Hall, for her life, and when she died it was to pass to her daughter, Elizabeth, afterwards Lady Barnard. The size and importance of the house is indicated by its being chosen as a temporary residence for Charles the First's queen, Henrietta Maria, who kept her court there for three weeks from June the 22nd to July the 3rd in 1643 in the early days of the Civil War. When Lady Barnard died childless in 1653 the house was sold to Sir Edward Walker, who gave it to his daughter and son-in-law, Sir John Clopton. The latter bequeathed it to his younger son, Sir Hugh Clopton, who lived the latter part of his life there and died a very old man in 1751. He was the one who carefully repaired and remodelled the old house, adding a modern eighteenth-century front. He did not demolish the original house, as has sometimes been stated. In 1753 his executors sold it to the Rev. Francis Gastrell, vicar of Frodsham in Cheshire.[1]

Gastrell had no interest in the Shakespearean associations of his property and was annoyed when an occasional

[1] R. B. Wheler, *History and Antiquities of Stratford-upon-Avon*, 1806, 135–6.

B

visitor asked to see the house and the garden with the mulberry tree. This had become a huge and magnificent specimen, a hundred and forty-seven years old, when in 1756 he decided that by overshadowing the house it made it too damp and dark and ordered it to be cut down and chopped into firewood. When the people of Stratford learned this some of them grew so incensed that they went to New Place, broke the windows and threatened violence to the clergyman and his family, if he did not quickly leave Stratford. He was so frightened that he complied. His wife was from Lichfield, one of the well-known Aston sisters who were close friends of Dr Johnson. The Gastrells had always spent part of the year in Lichfield; now they went back there.

But Stratford suffered further from the ill will of the Rev. Mr Gastrell. He did not sell New Place; he no longer lived there himself, but he kept servants there all the year round. Therefore, he was supposed to pay the monthly taxes levied on property owners for the maintenance of the poor, which he had thought he would escape by now living in Lichfield. He complained that the assessment was too high, and it is just possible that, in their resentment, the authorities may have increased the valuation of the property. He finally got so angry that he swore he would be assessed no more, went back to Stratford in 1759 and proceeded to have the house demolished and the timbers and materials sold, whereupon he left Stratford 'amidst the rage and curses of the inhabitants'.[1] He kept the site, which his widow finally sold in 1775. One important Shakespeare landmark was thus irretrievably lost.

It was natural that repercussions of this affair should

[1] R. B. Wheler, *History and Antiquities of Stratford-upon-Avon*, 1806, 138.

soon reach London. Angry letters and articles appeared in the newspapers and the magazines, and the story of the cutting down of the mulberry tree was revived at this time. The greater part of the wood from the tree had been bought by a Stratford watch and clockmaker, Thomas Sharp, an excellent wood-carver, who conceived the idea of carving small objects, such as boxes, bowls, ladles, goblets, tobacco-stoppers, and many other things from the wood and selling them to Shakespeare admirers.[1] The Stratford corporation bought some of the best logs for their own special use.[2] Among Garrick's papers for 1762 is a receipt for payment for four logs from Shakespeare's mulberry tree. He had a rather heavy, carved chair made from these by Hogarth. When Mrs Garrick died the chair was sold and eventually found its way to the Folger Shakespeare Library in Washington, where it is on exhibition.

In 1764 there had been some vague talk about a possible commemoration in Stratford of the bi-centennial year of Shakespeare's birth, but Garrick was abroad, and as nobody could be found to organize the celebration, the idea was quickly abandoned.

In 1767 the Stratford Corporation rebuilt its town-hall and was anxious to obtain a gift of a statue of Shakespeare for an empty niche on the north side of the building. One of the town-councillors, Mr Francis Wheler, who was often in London and knew some of the literary people there, mentioned this desire to George Steevens, the editor of Shakespeare's plays. Steevens, who was one of Garrick's enemies, suggested that if they flattered Garrick enough he might well be pleased to

[1] R. B. Wheler, *History and Antiquities of Stratford-upon-Avon*, 1806, 137.
[2] Benjamin Victor, *History of the Theatres of London*, London, 1771, **3**, 203.

give Stratford a statue of Shakespeare. Wheler suggested in November 1767 that the Corporation might make Garrick an Honorary Burgess of Stratford and present him with a testimonial in a box made from Shakespeare's mulberry tree. The idea was well received, and Garrick was told by a friend about the intended honour.[1] He immediately sensed the possibility of making this future event at Stratford the occasion for holding a large, impressive festival in honour of his beloved Shakespeare and started thinking about how this could best be done. However, it was not till October the 11th, 1768, that the following resolution was passed by the Town Council:

... David Garrick, Esq. the great theatrical genius of the age, and who has done the highest honours to the memory of the immortal Shakespeare (a native of this place) was unanimously elected an honorary burgess of this Corporation, and his freedom was directed to be presented to him in a box to be made of the Mulberry-tree planted by Shakespeare's own hands. . . .[2]

When Garrick was privately told by Wheler of this, he offered, as had been hoped, to give a statue and also a painting of Shakespeare to the Corporation. He chose Benjamin Wilson's painting of *Shakespeare in his Study*, and ordered a leaden copy to be made of Scheemaker's statue of Shakespeare, executed for Lord Pembroke in 1765, actually a somewhat revised version of the sculptor's statue of Shakespeare in Westminster Abbey which had been erected in 1741.[3] Wheler did not put

[1] Margaret Barton, *Garrick*. The Macmillan Company, New York, 1949, 202–3.

[2] James Boaden, *The Private Correspondence of David Garrick*, 2 vols. 1831–32, I, 323.

[3] Barton, op. cit., 205.

New Place with Guildhall and Chapel

(from R. B. Wheler's *History and Antiquities of Stratford*)

The Mulberry Box
(now in the British Museum)

the earlier proposal into writing till December 6, 1768, when he wrote the following flattering letter to Garrick:

Sir,

The old Town-hall of Stratford on Avon, where you very well know Shakespeare was born and lies buried, hath this present year been rebuilt by the Corporation, assisted by a liberal contribution from the nobility and gentry in the neighbourhood. The lower part of the building is used as a market-place, and is of great benefit to the poorer sort of people; over it is a handsome assembly room. It would be a reflection on the town of Stratford to have any public building erected there without some ornamental memorial of their immortal townsman; and the Corporation would be happy in receiving from your hands some statue, bust or picture of him, to be placed within this building. They would be equally pleased to have some picture of yourself, that the memory of both may be perpetuated together in that place which gave him birth, and where he still lives in the mind of every inhabitant.

The Corporation of Stratford, ever desirous of expressing their gratitude to all who do honour and justice to the memory of Shakespeare, and highly sensible that no person in any age hath excelled you therein, would think themselves much honoured if you would become one of their body. Though this borough doth not send members to parliament, perhaps the inhabitants may not be the less virtuous; and to render the freedom of such a place the more agreeable to you, the Corporation propose to send it in a box made of that very mulberry-tree planted by Shakespeare's own hand. The story of that valuable relic is too long to be here inserted; but Mr. Kea[te], who is so obliging as to convey this to you, will acquaint you therewith, and the writer hereof flatters himself it will afford you some entertainment, and at the same time convince you that the inhabitants of Stratford are worthy of your notice.

I am your obedient, humble servant,

Frans. Wheler.[1]

[1] Boaden, op. cit., I, 322–3.

It took a long time to carve the mulberry box, and it was May 1769 before it was ready and an official presentation of the freedom of the borough could be made. On May the 3rd the Corporation sent the following letter to Garrick:

SIR,

THE Mayor, Alderman, and Burgesses of the ancient Borough of Stratford-upon-Avon – a town, that glories in giving birth to the immortal Shakespeare, whose memory you have so highly honoured, and whose conception you have ever so happily expressed – rejoice in an opportunity of adding their mite to that universal applause your inimitable powers have most justly merited; and as a mark of their esteem and gratitude have respectfully transmitted to you the Freedom of their Borough in a box made from a Mulberry-tree undoubtedly planted by Shakespeare's own hand, which they hope you will do them the honour of accepting.

By order of the Mayor, Alderman, and Burgesses in Common Council,

> Signed by
> WM. HUNT, Town Clerk.[1]

On May the 8th Garrick wrote the following gracious letter of acceptance:

GENTLEMEN,

I CANNOT sufficiently express my acknowledgements for the honour you have done me in electing me a Burgess of Stratford-upon-Avon; a town which will be ever distinguished and reverenced as the birth-place of Shakespeare.

There are many circumstances which have greatly added to the obligation you have conferred upon me. The freedom of your town given to me unanimously, sent to me in such an elegant and

[1] *The London Chronicle*, May 9–11, 1769, 25, 446, 2–3.

inestimable box, and delivered to me in so flattering a manner, merit my warmest gratitude. It will be impossible for me ever to forget those who have honoured me so much as to mention my unworthy name with that of their immortal townsman.

I am, Gentlemen,
Your most obliged and obedient humble servant,
D. GARRICK [1]

Finally, on May the 11th the proper officers of the Stratford Corporation waited on Garrick at his house in Southampton Street and presented the freedom of the borough in the mulberry box, an event that was duly noted the same day in the newspapers, with the added information:

In consequence of the above, a jubilee in honour and to the memory of Shakespeare will be appointed at Stratford the beginning of September which will be kept up every seventh year. Mr. Garrick, at the particular request of the Corporation, has accepted the Stewardship. At the first jubilee, a large handsome edifice, lately erected in Stratford by subscription, will be named Shakespeare's Hall, and dedicated to his memory. [2]

A detailed description of the mulberry box appeared a few days later:

The ornaments on the box of very nice workmanship . . . are on the front, *Fame* holding the bust of Shakespeare, and the three graces crowning him with laurels, prettily displayed; on the ends emblematical figures representing tragedy and comedy; on the back part Mr. Garrick in the character of Lear, in the storm scene; and the top and corners were ornamented with devices of Shakespeare's works, all curiously carved and highly finished by an eminent carver in Birmingham. The four feet are silver griffins with garnet eyes. The Corporation paid T. Davies the eminent carver from Birmingham £55 for his work.

---

[1] *The London Chronicle*, May 13–16, 1769, **25**, 458, 2.
[2] Ibid., May 9–11, 1769, **25**, 446, 3.

The mulberry box is now in the possession of the British Museum, on permanent exhibition.[1]

The Corporation also sent a complimentary letter to George Keate, thanking him for his trouble in attending Mr Garrick, and presented him with a writing standish, made of wood from the mulberry tree and richly mounted in silver 'as an acknowledgement for his very elegant and spirited defence of the first of poets in his *Ferney*, an epistle in verse to Monsieur de Voltaire . . . it shows their desire to reward literary as well as scenic merit where they find it connected with Shakespeare'.[2]

On May the 18th *The London Chronicle* provided more details about the coming event:

We hear the new edifice in Stratford, intended to be called Shakespeare's Hall, will be decorated in the most elegant manner before the Jubilee in September, and that the Corporation have prevailed on Mr. Garrick to sit for his picture, which they will put up at one end of the large room; and that Mr. Garrick will present the town with a picture of Shakespeare for the other end. Great preparations are making for the oratorio in the church, the dedication of the room to the immortal memory of Shakespeare, and for the grand fireworks upon the river.[3]

The Corporation commissioned from Thomas Gainsborough a portrait of Garrick for which they paid sixty guineas. He painted Garrick standing with his arm around a pillar holding a bust of Shakespeare (see Frontispiece). Mrs Garrick is said to have considered this the best portrait of her husband. Unfortunately both this

[1] Hugh Tait, 'Garrick, Shakespeare and Wilkes', *The British Museum Quarterly*, Dec. 1961, **24**, 100–7.

[2] *The Oxford Magazine*, June 1769, **2**, 234. Keate, an intimate acquaintance of Voltaire, had published *Ferney; an Epistle to Voltaire* in the previous year.

[3] *The London Chronicle*, May 13–16, 1769, **25**, 458, 2.

and Wilson's picture of *Shakespeare in his Study* were destroyed in a fire at the Stratford Town Hall in 1946.

Obviously the planning was going ahead rapidly. On May the 18th the first public statement made by Garrick about the coming jubilee occurred in an epilogue, composed and spoken by himself, for his last appearance of the season of 1768–69 at the Drury Lane Theatre. He promised to return for the next season, and continued:

> My eyes, till then, no sights like these will see,
> Unless we meet at Shakespeare's Jubilee!
> On Avon's *Banks, where flowers eternal blow*!
> Like its full stream our Gratitude shall flow!
> Then let us revel, show our fond regard,
> On that lov'd Spot, first breathed our *matchless* Bard;
> To Him all Honour, Gratitude is due,
> To Him we owe our all — To *Him* and *You*.[1]

On June the 15th more news appeared in *The St James Chronicle*:

We hear that Dr. Arne, who has the Merit of having contributed his Mite towards the Embellishment of the inimitable Works of Shakespeare, by adapting his Music to all the principal Songs in his Plays, has generously offered his Service in directing the Musical Performances intended to be exhibited at Stratford-upon-Avon in September next, in Honour of that inimitable Dramatic Writer's Memory and to set to Music a new Ode which will be written for the Occasion, and executed in a Manner intirely new. And we hear that the Doctor's Offers are kindly accepted.[2]

Garrick was confident that the Jubilee would draw several thousand visitors to Stratford besides the large number of people that would participate in the different

---

[1] Joseph Knight, *David Garrick*, London, 1894, 245–6.
[2] *The St James Chronicle*, June 10, 1769, 4, col. 4.

events. He counted on using the singers and the full orchestra from Drury Lane for the musical events and would need one hundred and seventy participants in costume for the ambitious procession and pageant he had in mind. Of course Drury Lane's technical staff, carpenters, and other workmen would also be needed. All these people, as well as the visitors, would have to be housed and fed — a gigantic undertaking in a small market town of less than three thousand inhabitants and with only one inn, the White Lion; stabling would also have to be arranged for all the horses that brought the visitors to town, and most important, a large temporary building, big enough to accommodate about two thousand people, would have to be erected for the meetings, dinners, and assemblies that were in prospect. The Corporation agreed to bear the expenses in connexion with the erection of such a building.[1]

After permission had been obtained from Lord Dorset, the owner, a large tract of land on the river bank near the bridge was cleared; more than one hundred trees were cut down upon Bamstead Mead, opening up a good view;[2] it was decided to erect the building needed there quite close to the river, and to model it on the famous Rotunda in Ranelagh Gardens, the plans for which had been drawn in 1742 by James Lacy, Garrick's co-manager at Drury Lane. It was planned as an octagonal amphitheatre, 120 feet in diameter (a little smaller than the Rotunda, which had a diameter of 140 feet), to be built of wood and with a dome supported by 'a colonade of the Corinthian order, distant about ten

---

[1] Isabel R. Mann, 'The Garrick Jubilee at Stratford upon Avon', *The Shakespeare Quarterly*, I, 131.

[2] *The London Chronicle*, July 21–24, 1769, 26, 75, 1.

feet from the sides'.[1] As at the Rotunda there was to be
an orchestra at one end, large enough to hold the Drury
Lane band, the singers, and the Shakespeare statue. The
room was to be lighted by a magnificent chandelier,
holding eight hundred lights. Garrick came down to
Stratford for a short visit when the building was started
and left the further supervision of its erection to his
brother, George Garrick, and Mr Latimore, both of

The Amphitheatre
(from *The Gentleman's Magazine*, Sept. 1769)

whom were employed in the offices of administration at
the Drury Lane Theatre. The outside of the building
was not very prepossessing, judging from a picture of it
in *The Gentleman's Magazine* for September 1769 (see
above). But later many people commented most favourably on the elegance of the large room with the gilt bases
and capitals of the columns and the painted ceilings, and
found everything there in excellent taste. The building
became known as *The Amphitheatre* or *The Great Booth*.

[1] *The Gentleman's Magazine*, Sept. 1769, **39**, 422.

But the workmen brought down from London were faced with many troubles and delays. Joseph Cradock visiting Stratford less than two weeks before the opening of the Jubilee found great confusion. A very pessimistic guide showing him the unfinished building said, 'for the completion of which, the boards are not yet arrived, and so far from it, they are not even yet bargained for at Birmingham'. He also mentioned that the lamps for the illumination of the building, sent from the Drury Lane Theatre by wagons, arrived all broken, 'if ever they left Drury Lane in safety, you see they are here all shivered to pieces'.[1] Some of the London workmen he saw were equally unhappy, saying:

'We are sent down here to make some preparations for the entertainment, but we are absolutely without materials, and we can gain no assistance whatever from the inhabitants, who are all fearfull of lending us any article whatever. We would do any thing in the world to serve our good Master, but he is entirely kept in the dark, as to the situation of every thing here, and we only wish to return to London again as soon as possible to save expenses.'[2]

But finally all obstacles were overcome, and the Great Booth was ready for the opening.

Kitchen facilities were built near by, and Mr Peyton, the host of the White Lion Inn, took over the catering. He sent an order to London for 300 dozen pewter plates, 300 dozen knives and forks, 100 dozen pewter spoons, 10 pipes of wine, 50 dozen stewpans and kettles, and 300 waiters.[3] Large supplies of food were brought in,

---

[1] Joseph Cradock, *Literary and Miscellaneous Memories*, London, 1826, **1**, 212.

[2] Ibid., **1**, 213.

[3] *Lloyd's Evening Post*, Sept. 6–8, 1769, **25**, 234, 2.

including a turtle weighing 150 lb., and numerous cooks were engaged who started preparing the food more than a week ahead of the opening. A fixed price of 3*s*. 6*d*. was set for the ordinary dinner, including wine, to be served at the Great Booth. Public breakfasts, price 1*s*., were to be served at the Town-hall, which could accommodate about 800 people.

Housing the visitors presented considerable difficulty. On August the 8th a newspaper noted that 'upon a Report of the Difficulty of getting Beds at the ensuing Jubilee . . . several Gentlemen have made Parties to pitch Tents in the common Field for their Accommodation'.[1] The White Lion Inn was swamped with requests for accommodation, which could not be met. Rooms had to be found in town, and many were poorly equipped. On September the 2nd a visitor wrote that the upholsterers of London 'have furnished every house here and in the environs with new beds (in some sixteen or twenty) and other neat furniture, and agree with every person who has rooms and no bedding, etc., to fit them up and share the profits which has made the lodgings plenty'.[2] The rate was fixed at a guinea a night for a bed.

At the White Lion Inn the common rooms were labelled for the occasion '*Hamlet*, *King Lear*, *Richard*, *Macbeth*, *Othello*, *Measure for Measure*, etc. and the humorous device on the larder was *As You Like It*'.[3] When Cradock discussed the coming Jubilee with some of the most prominent burghers they were uneasy and afraid

[1] *The St James Chronicle*, Aug. 5–8, 1769, 4, col. 3.
[2] *The London Chronicle*, Sept. 5–7, 1769, **26**, 238, 1.
[3] *The London Evening Post*, Aug. 31, 1769. All references to this newspaper are to clippings found in *Collectanea*, **2**, at the Folger Shakespeare Library.

of the consequences of the great invasion of visitors and would have been glad, but for the risk to their homes, to leave Stratford during the Jubilee. They were certain that 'the Peytons had just reason to be under the greatest apprehensions; that they were good people and would be ready to do anything in their power to accommodate old customers, but they could not receive even the twentieth part of those that had applied to them; and in case of a disturbance they should have all their plate stolen and their furniture destroyed'.[1] The burghers also asked Mr Cradock, since he was an acquaintance of Garrick's, to write to him immediately and give him a full and truthful account of the situation to warn him about the difficulties. This he did.

Unfortunately Garrick did not always get the co-operation and support he needed for this great under-taking, and far too many problems, both minor and major, were referred to him for solution. He had one close friend, who was always willing to listen to him and advise him, Domenico Angelo, a well-educated Italian, who had settled in London and was famous as a fashion-able teacher of riding and fencing there. He was both handsome and exceedingly graceful and was considered one of the most elegant men of his time. As a young man he had been in Venice, where he had known Canaletto, who was the best scene-painter of his time. From him he had acquired a wide knowledge of stage machinery and the scenic decoration of the stage. All this he dis-cussed with Garrick and had on several occasions helped him with technical innovations. He was also an expert on fireworks and volunteered his services as chief en-gineer of the fireworks to be used at Stratford. His son

[1] Cradock, op. cit., I, 213–14.

Henry, at that time a boy of nine, writes in his *Reminiscences*:

... I though then a boy was present at many councils held at my father's house, in Carlisle-street, for the planning and regulating of this spectacle, in honour of the bard of Avon. I think I see my father ... as he stood directing his engineers in the fabrication of *rockets*, *crackers*, *catherine-wheels* and *squibs*, to play off at Stratford.[1]

Fireworks were planned for the three evenings of the Jubilee. *The Weekly Magazine* for August the 19th–26th quoted a letter from Stratford stating, 'It is incredible what a number of people flock here to view the preparations for the jubilee. Two wagon-loads of fireworks, etc., made under the inspection of Mr. Angelo, are arrived here from London. A quantity of very beautiful lamps, of various colours, for the illumination, are also come.'[2]

These lamps were to be used in another project planned by Garrick and Angelo, the illumination of important places in Stratford at night and the erecting of so-called transparencies – large paintings on framed transparent silk-screens, at night illuminated from behind. Angelo had seen these used effectively at a carnival in Venice and had helped Garrick to install them for some of his ballets at Drury Lane.[3] Such large illuminated transparencies, representing Painting, Sculpture and Architecture, had on June the 4th, the King's birthday, been used to decorate the outside of the Royal Academy; they were painted by members and much

---

[1] Henry Angelo, *Reminiscences*, London, 1828, 1, 41.
[2] *The Weekly Magazine*, or *Edinburgh Amusement*, 5, 286, 2.
[3] Angelo, op. cit., 1, 10–14.

admired.[1] Garrick thought he might be able to borrow these for the Jubilee and wrote to the President and Council of the Royal Academy about it.

'But they refused to lend them and gave the following very sensible reasons for not complying: that they had received them, for a particular occasion, from some very ingenious men of their own body, and therefore could not part with them in compliment to these gentlemen. Besides, there were many artists possessed of great genius, in indigent circumstances, who might be procured at an easy rate, and to whom it would be of service, that would do something more applicable to the intended purpose and more in honour to Shakespeare than the figures of painting, sculpture and architecture could possibly be.'[2]

Garrick and Angelo had to engage their own painters, whose work was later much admired. Boswell gives a most enthusiastic, detailed account of these transparencies:

I am surprised that your Correspondents who have so justly praised Mr. Angelo's Fireworks, have not mentioned the Pictures on the Bank of the Avon, fronting the Amphitheatre. There we beheld Time leading Shakespeare to Immortality, Tragedy on one Side and Comedy on the other, copied from the fine Ideas of Sir Joshua Reynolds. Behind these Pictures were placed a Number of Lamps, which gave them a most beautiful Transparency. In the same Style were five Pictures in the Windows of the Town-hall: In the Middle Shakespeare, in the Attitude of exclaiming, 'Oh! for a Muse of Fire!' On the Windows on one Side of him, Lear and Caliban: On the Windows on the other Side, Sir John Falstaff and Ancient Pistol. In the same Style too was a Piece of Painting hung before the Windows of the Room where Shakespeare was born, representing the Sun breaking through the Clouds.[3]

[1] *The Gentleman's Magazine,* June 1769, **39,** 315–16.
[2] *The London Evening Post,* Oct. 10, 1769.
[3] *The Public Advertiser,* Sept. 16, 1769, 2, col. 2.

Another writer states that 'it was affixed to the Front of the House, with the following Inscription:

Here dying Clouds contend with growing Light.

SHAKESPEARE'.[1]

In the painting of 'the Sun struggling through Clouds to enlighten the World . . . was figuratively delineated the low Circumstances of Shakespeare, from which his Strength of Genius rais'd him, to become the *Glory of his Country*'.[2]

Arrangements were also made for the placing of thirty cannon (thirty-two pounders as well as mortars) on the river bank. They were to be fired to mark the opening of the Jubilee and at appropriate moments later.

The roads leading to Stratford that would be heavily travelled by visitors were not in very good repair and needed improvement. A letter from Stratford written August the 14th gives an interesting account of this:

. . . The Gentlemen of the Country seem also to have interested themselves in the Business of the Jubilee, and to have all taken a Share in the great Undertaking. For in order to accelerate and render the Resort of the Company to this extraordinary Jubilee easy and commodious to all the Gentry from Wolverhampton, Shrewsbury, Chester and Ireland (from whence great Numbers of Persons of the first Distinction are expected, many Houses being already taken for them) the Commissioners of the new Turnpikes from Dudley to Stratford, have employed a great Number of extraordinary Hands to complete that very useful and beneficial Road . . . the Advantages of which extend to the Metropolis itself, it would not probably have been completed till the next Spring, had not the Eagerness of the Country Gentlemen

---

[1] *The Public Advertiser*, Sept. 16, 1769, 3, col. 1.
[2] Victor, op. cit., 3, 207.

C

in the Commission, to contribute in some Degree to the Honour,
and to perpetuate the Memory of the immortal Shakespeare,
induced them to set on an extraordinary Number of Hands to get
it ready for this great Occasion, so as to render the Means of
Resort to the Stratford Jubilee more easy and commodious: For
that Purpose the Gentlemen, at the several Divisions of the Road,
have taken their different Shares of superintending and completing
it ... to be in Readiness for that great Solemnity i.e. the Jubilee;
on which Occasion also the Road is intended to be honoured with
the Name of the *Shakespeare Road*.[1]

For the Jubilee 'a medal engraved by Mr Westwood
of Birmingham, similar to that worn by Mr. Garrick,
was struck ... in copper, silver, and gold'.[2] Several of
these medals are preserved in the Folger Shakespeare
Library in Washington. Boswell reports: 'We all wore,
hung in a blue Ribband at our Breasts, a Medal of
Shakespeare' and describes it:

On one Side was the Head of Shakespeare and round it this
Inscription,

WE SHALL NOT LOOK UPON HIS LIKE AGAIN

And on the Reverse:

JUBILEE
AT STRATFORD
IN HONOUR
AND TO THE
MEMORY OF
SHAKESPEARE,
SEPT. 1769
D. G.
STEWARD[3]

[1] *The Public Advertiser*, Aug. 18, 1769, 2, col. 3.
[2] Wheler, op. cit., 169.
[3] *The Public Advertiser*, Sept. 16, 1769, 2, col. 2.

Many-coloured Jubilee ribbons, to be made into favours, were made in Coventry to be sold at the Jubilee. Boswell mentions that the shop-bills advertising them 'were Pieces of Genius. Mr. Jackson, from Tavistock-street, London, gave about the following one:

SHAKESPEARE'S JUBILEE

A RIBBAND has been made on Purpose at Coventry, called the *Shakespeare Ribband*: it is in Imitation of the Rain-bow, which uniting the Colours of all Parties, is likewise an Emblem of the great Variety of his Genius.

'Each Change of many-coloured Life he drew.'

JOHNSON.

Boswell further comments, 'I dare say Mr. Samuel Johnson never imagined that this fine Verse of his would appear on a Bill to promote the Sale of Rib-bands.'[1]

Thomas Sharp, the Stratford man who had bought most of the wood from Shakespeare's mulberry tree, carved from it such a large number of small souvenirs to be sold in the streets during the Jubilee that insinuations were made that he had purchased other mulberry wood or he would not have been able to make so many articles. The accusations of fraud worried him, and years later, during his last illness, 'he called in the Mayor and one of the standing Justices of the Peace for the borough, and ordered a friend to draw up an affidavit, wishing to convince the world to the contrary of such insinuations and enable him to set a proper value upon the relics of the celebrated tree. The affidavit was voluntarily made.'[2] He confirmed it with his oath.

[1] *The Public Advertiser*, Sept. 16, 1769, 2, col. 2.
[2] Wheler, op. cit., 137.

No attempts were made to decorate the large church, inside or outside, except for Shakespeare's tombstone in the church floor and his monument on the wall. The latter had been repaired and repainted in 1746, but the paint was probably freshened up for the Jubilee; one visitor remarked that 'the poet's bust on his monument was so loaded with branches of bays, which they call laurel, as to appear similar only to the God Pan in an old picture'.[1] Mrs Garrick and Mrs Barthelemon, a young singer, decorated Shakespeare's tombstone with flowers and evergreens before the opening of the Jubilee. A letter dated May 31st, 1769, which Garrick received with a gift of a pair of gloves, refers to the earlier repair of the monument. The writer was John Ward, the actor-manager of the strolling provincial company, which played in Stratford in 1746. (His daughter married another provincial actor-manager, by name Roger Kemble, and became the mother of the well-known London actor-manager John Philip Kemble and the famous actress, Mrs Siddons.) He wrote as follows:

Dear Sir,

On reading the newspapers I find you are preparing a grand Jubilee, to be kept at Stratford upon Avon, to the Memory of the Immortal Shakespeare. I have sent you a pair of gloves which have often covered his hands: they were made me a present by a descendant of the family, when myself and company went over there from Warwick, in the year 1746, to perform the play of 'Othello', as a benefit, for repairing his monument in the great church, which we did gratis, the whole of the receipts being expended upon that alone.

[1] *The Gentleman's Magazine*, Sept. 1769, 39, 422.

The person who gave them to me, William Shakespeare by name, assured me his father had often declared to him, they were the identical gloves of our great poet . . .[1]

James Boaden, the editor of Garrick's *Private Correspondence*, in a footnote expresses his doubt about the authenticity of the gloves mentioned in the letter. A newspaper note after the jubilee speaks of a gift of two pairs of gloves made to Garrick but without mentioning the name of the donor:

Since the intention of the Jubilee in honour of Shakespeare has been in agitation, a great number of curiosities and relics, relative to the great and first-born son of Nature, have been presented to Mr. Garrick, and among others two pairs of gloves, well attested to have been worn by Shakespeare on the stage; the one his tragedy, and the other his comedy gloves. Formerly no actor appeared on the stage (unless in some very low character indeed) without gloves; and those for tragedy were much more rich and pompous than those for comedy.[2]

The programme for the three-day festival was carefully planned to appeal to the general public as well as to the fashionable world. What strikes a modern reader of the programme is the strange fact that no performance of a Shakespeare play was included. There is no indication that Garrick ever considered the production of a Shakespeare play at the jubilee, although surely some of his friends must have expected one. Actually as early as May the 25th the following verse appeared in a newspaper:

[1] Boaden, op. cit., 1, 352–3.
[2] *The London Evening Post*, Sept. 16, 1769.

To Mr. Garrick upon the intended Jubilee in Honour of Shakespeare.

To shew in all its Glory Shakespeare's Fame
To give a *Jubilee* deserves the Name
To give all Honour to his Memory due
Produce his Dramas realiz'd by you.

B.R.[1]

Certainly some of the entertainments planned had nothing whatsoever to connect them with Shakespeare. There was to be an Assembly Ball on the first and the third nights. On August the 31st the following notice appeared in the newspapers: 'Ladies are desired to be at the ball on the 6th either in negligée or in full dress, as they please.'[2]

For the second night a masquerade was planned. The first announcement of this appeared in the papers on August the 2nd and was repeated at regular intervals during the month. The coming masquerade caught the fancy of Society and became the talk of London. On August the 27th George Montagu wrote to his friend, Horace Walpole, who was in Paris: "'Tis inconceivable the preparations that are making at Stratford by that simpleton Garrick; all the women are tearing the clothes off their backs to convert them into jubilee masquerade habits.'[3] During August some curious advertisements appeared in the newspapers. Obviously some of these notices were facetious, others serious. A few examples follow:

---

[1] *The St James Chronicle*, May 23–25, 1769, 4, col. 1.
[2] *The London Evening Post*, Aug. 31, 1769.
[3] Horace Walpole, *Correspondence*. Edited by W. S. Lewis. New Haven 1941, 10, 287.

SHAKESPEARE

Whereas PHILIP CARR, Peruke-Maker of Devereux Court in the Strand, hath purchased, at a great Expence, several Wig-Blocks made out of the famous MULBERRY TREE of STRATFORD, he takes the earliest Opportunity of acquainting his Customers (especially those Gentlemen of the Law who discover in themselves an Inclination to become Poets) that he will furnish them with Wigs of all Kinds at the usual Prices, though he would humbly recommend Tyes, on the present Occasion, as being fuller of Hair, and consequently more capable of retaining the inspiring Quality of that sacred Wood.[1]

MASQUERADE

Any Ladies or Gentlemen desirous of making up Habits against the Approaching Masquerade at Stratford upon Avon, or any other Occasion, may see select and choice Collection of original Drawings for the Purpose, containing a great Variety of agreeable Characters and may at a very Easy Expence have the Advertiser's Opinion and Superintendence in making up the Dresses, he having great Experience and some Taste in those Affairs, by applying at or opposite Mr. Wright's Haberdasher, Glanville-street, the upper End of Rathbone Place, facing Soho Square.[2]

SHAKESPEARE JUBILEE BALL and MASQUERADE

The Curious in Fancy Dress may be served with the Bark of a Tree, that resembles a beautiful Lace, by applying to Mrs. Williams, Peter-Street, Bloomsbury. N.B. No person whose Business is making up of Dresses need apply, as none but Nobility and those of Rank and Fashion will be served.[3]

Tickets to the masquerade were priced at half a guinea.

In order to draw the people interested in sports to the Jubilee a horse race was planned for the third day. This

---

[1] *The Public Advertiser*, Aug. 7, 1769, 1, col. 1.
[2] Ibid., Aug. 9, 1769, 3, col. 3.
[3] Ibid., Aug. 16, 1769, 1, col. 3.

was first mentioned in a newspaper on August the 14th:

We hear that the Noblemen and Gentlemen in and near Stratford-upon-Avon, have generously subscribed for a Plate to be run for on Friday the 8th of September, which will make the Jubilee in Honour of Shakespeare continue three Days, viz. Wednesday the 6th, Thursday the 7th, and Friday the 8th of September. We hope to be able in a few Days to give the particular Entertainments.[1]

The race was announced in the papers on August the 24th:

JUBILEE RACE, at Stratford upon Avon

A Jubilee Cup, value 5ol. (whereon will be engraved Shakespeare's arms, with other proper decorations) will be run for on Shottery Meadow, near Stratford upon Avon, on Friday the 8th day of September next, by four-year-old horses, etc. and those which never won 5ol. to carry 8 st., those that have won 5ol. to carry 8 st. 4 l. and those that have won two 5ol. to carry 8 st. 8 l. and those which have won three 5ol. to carry 8 st. 12 l. and all of superior qualifications to carry 2 l. more, the best of three heats, each heat to be three miles.

To enter for the cup on Monday the 4th of September, at the house of Mr. Judd in Stratford, between the hours of two and six, and to be subject to the article which will be produced.

Every horse etc., that enters for this cup, to pay one guinea entrance, and five shillings to the clerk of the course, and to subscribe 2l. 2s. towards further diversions. . . . The horses to start at 12 o'clock.

The horses to stand at the house of Mr. Judd only from the day of entrance to the time of running.

No less than three reputed running horses to start for this cup. . . .

No horse, etc. to start for this cup that is not plated by a smith, that has subscribed 10s. 6d. towards it. . . . All differences in entering and running to be determined by the majority of subscribers present.

N.B. The course upon this most delightful meadow (allowed

---

[1] *The St James Chronicle*, Aug. 12–15, 1769, 4, col. 3.

to be one of the finest in the kingdom) has been altered and made more convenient and agreeable both for horses and spectators; indeed there was very little occasion for art, where nature has done so much; the stream of the surrounding Avon, the verdant lawns, and the rising hills and woods, form a most agreeable scene.[1]

The most elaborate, spectacular, and ambitious entertainment was planned for the second day, namely a grand procession of

170 persons (chiefly represented by performers from the theatres in London) properly dressed, in all the principal characters to be met with in Shakespeare's plays; with a large and highly ornamented triumphal car, in which two persons, representing Melpomene and Thalia, with the Graces, were to be drawn by six persons habited like satyrs, with attendants carrying emblematic devices and insignia, and accompanied by the whole band of vocal and instrumental music, to perform a serenade at Shakespeare's statue and crown it with a wreath of laurel.[2]

The problem of providing costumes for all the characters in the procession, where nineteen plays were represented, was solved by the borrowing of the greater part of the wardrobe from the Drury Lane theatre. In a letter written September the 2nd a visitor reports:

There are upwards of 150 large boxes of dresses and scenery, which we imagine are for the procession that will follow Shakespeare's effigy and Mr. Garrick, when drawn through the town in the triumphal cars.[3]

The proper assignments of parts to so many people must have been exceedingly difficult. For instance, the actor William (Gentleman) Smith was asked to walk as

---

[1] *The London Evening Post*, Aug. 24, 1769.
[2] Wheler, op. cit., 186, footnote.
[3] *The London Evening Post*, Sept. 7, 1769.

Benedick in the procession, but was very unhappy about it.[1] Garrick changed his part and received the following letter from him on August the 16th:

Dear Sir,

Your politeness has entirely removed my *awkwardness*, and I am totally at your disposal. The post and dress you allot for me will be most agreeable to me, and all scruples are removed. If I recollect right, the hat I wear in Richard is very shabby; and the little ornaments I wore in it are locked up in town under a key I have with me. The hat that Mr. Powell used in King John is a good one, and I should suppose might be had with the ornaments on it; [William Powell had died on July 7, 1769] if not, I should be glad of yours. You must excuse my mentioning these particulars, as the motive is that I may appear to the best advantage in your train. . . . I hope your fears of ill-consequences from the fatigues, which must be great, will prove groundless. . . . Will your hurry allow you time to tell me where I am to go in Stratford? and whether you mean to apply to our manager for Richard's dress or would have me do it. I think they will make less difficulty with you than me? On what day ought I to be at Stratford?[2]

There are a few references to other parts assigned, such as: 'We hear the character of Sir John Falstaff, who is to be drawn in the procession in a car, is to be presented by Signor Grimaldi.'[3] Henry Angelo tells us that he was to walk as Ariel; his father as Mark Antony, and Mrs Yates, a well-known actress, as Cleopatra.[4] The participants were supposed to gather in the large school, known as the College, and to walk from there through the town to the Amphitheatre.

[1] *Garrickiana*, 1, 145. The Folger Shakespeare Library.
[2] Boaden, op. cit., 1, 363–4.
[3] *The London Evening Post*, Aug. 31, 1769.
[4] Angelo, op. cit., 1, 48.

As the first serious entertainment of the opening day Dr Arne's celebrated oratorio *Judith* was to be performed in the large church with the composer conducting. The programme planned for the first day was described in the newspapers on August the 16th:

At Twelve, the Ladies, being either half or fully dressed, go to the Church, where an Oratorio will be performed. From the Church the Band in grand Chorus will proceed to the Great Booth, where Dinner will be prepared, after that Songs, Glees, etc., etc., will fill up the Time till the Ode is performed; the Recitative Part by Mr. Garrick, who will crown a Statue of Shakespeare with Laurel. The Ode is long and excellent in its Way; the Music is composed by Dr. Arne, who, I hear, has succeeded happily.[1]

Garrick had hoped that one of the university poets would be willing to write an ode for the occasion, but they refused to do so. Garrick himself was known as a fairly able writer of prologues, epilogues, and light verse, but he hesitated to undertake anything as ambitious as an occasional ode. His friend, Mr J. Sharp of Cambridge, who hoped to attend the Jubilee, wrote to Garrick on May the 20th:

I hope you will furnish something better in the memory of the latter [i.e. Shakespeare] at his jubilee, than Mr. Martyn's and Mr. Neel's prologue and epilogue at his benefit in the year 1738, for erecting his monument in Westminster Abbey . . . I met Mr. G[ray] here at dinner last Sunday; he spoke handsomely of your happy knack at epilogues . . . but he calls the Stratford Jubilee, Vanity Fair.[2]

---

[1] *The Public Advertiser*, Aug. 16, 1769, 3, col. 1.
[2] Boaden, op. cit., I, 349.

Garrick did receive the offer of an ode from William Havard, who had long been a judicious actor of secondary parts in both tragedy and comedy at Drury Lane. He had recently retired from the theatre.[1] He wrote to Garrick on May the 30th:

... I give you joy, Sir, of your approaching Shakespearian Jubilee. The people of Stratford could not err in their choice of a President. — They had properly no other.

May I not be permitted, Sir, to be a walker in the cavalcade, and hold up the train of part of the ceremony? I have already written an Ode in honour of our great master, which you have formerly thought well of. Dr. Boyce has set it excellently to music; and voices, I should think, will not be wanting on this occasion; but you will determine all this yourself.[2]

However, Garrick decided not to use the ode. The disappointed author sent it to *The Public Advertiser*, where it was published on August the 8th under the following caption:

At the Time when the whole Nation is united in paying Honour to the Memory of the immortal Shakespeare, the following little Piece, tho' it appeared in our Paper some years ago, will we hope not be unacceptable to our Readers.

ODE to the Memory of SHAKESPEARE
written by Mr. HAVARD
And set to Music by Dr. BOYCE.[3]

A letter published in the same paper on July the 29th offered some ironic advice concerning the Dedication Ode and the ceremonies to follow it:

[1] Knight, op. cit., 242.
[2] Boaden, op. cit., I, 352.
[3] *The Public Advertiser*, Aug. 8, 1769, 4, col. 2.

As I intend being at the Stratford Jubilee, I should be very sorry to have the Ode resemble this [i.e. Gray's *Ode at the Installation at Cambridge*]. The subject is widely different from Mr. Gray's, and I beg and beseech the Poet who is to compose it, that it may mean something. . . . I would recommend to them [i.e. the planners] to follow any Thing that is Praiseworthy. I make no Doubt, therefore, but, upon a particular Enquiry they will approve and adopt the same regular Plan with which the Installation at Cambridge was conducted; which, whether we consider the Spirit and Dignity of the Speeches, the peculiar Politeness of the Proctors, or the singular Decency and Delicacy of the Under-Graduates to the Ladies, may be set up to all future Ceremonies as the Standard of good Sense, good Breeding, and good Manners.

I am, Sir,

Your humble Servant

PHILALETHES[1]

Garrick finally wrote the ode himself and called it *An Ode upon dedicating a Building, and erecting a Statue to Shakespeare, at Stratford-upon-Avon*. He may have approached the task somewhat reluctantly, but in the end he was pleased with the result. His friend, Joseph Cradock, saw him in Stratford before the presentation of the ode and reported:

The best circumstance was, that Garrick was well satisfied as to the correctness of the composition of the Ode; for he told me it had been fully examined, and ably criticised by his friend Dr. Wharton, but he felt that reciting an account of characters by day-light, instead of acting them in the evening, would not fully come up to the public expectation.[2]

After the recitation of the ode Garrick planned to deliver a prose eulogy of Shakespeare. A long letter

[1] *The Public Advertiser*, July 29, 1769, 2, col. 3.
[2] Cradock, op. cit., I, 217–18.

discussing this plan, dated August the 19th, appeared in a newspaper on August the 29th:

The approaching Festival at Stratford being the principal Object of public Attention, any Information relating to so magnificent a Solemnity, I apprehend, will prove acceptable to your Readers. To the Literati, I am sure, the Intelligence will be pleasing that the Pageantry, of which so pompous an Account has been given in the Papers, is solely calculated for the *Million*, who are capable of receiving Pleasure through the Medium of the Senses only; but a Dish of *Caviare* is prepared for such intellectual Spirits who are susceptible of more abstract and refined Indulgence. For the Entertainment of these our great *Roscius* proposes, on the first Day, to pronounce a Eulogium, in the Manner of Monsieur Fontenelle, on the wonderful dramatic Genius, in whose Honour the Company are assembled.   In this Composition he will take Occasion to enter, with great Precision, into the specific Excellencies of our incomparable Bard. He will develope, by a curious Investigation, those delicate Touches of Nature, which have set the Name of Shakespeare at the Head of all dramatic Writers: He will make a curious Discrimination of his Tragic from his Comic Powers, and probably ascertain the long contested Problem 'Whether Melpomene or Thalia derives most Honour from the Labours of the Avon Bard?' – He will demonstrate where his Idol has succeeded by a Deviation from the Rules of dramatic Writing, and point out in a clear and convincing Disquisition those Pieces which would have received additional Beauty by an Adherence to those Laws. This, it is said, will conclude the literary Entertainment of the first Day.

On the second Day, the great Vice-regent of Shakespeare will undertake a minute Examination of the Poet's Versification, which will lead him into a Discussion of the Harmony of his Numbers, the Knowledge of the Rhythmus, which he possessed and exercised in so eminent a Degree, and the wonderful Attention which he gave to the Variation of his Pauses. These Observations the great Artist will exemplify by reading several Passages, in which

Occasion will offer of pointing out, but with great good Nature, the Errors of some modern Performers, in Respect to Accent, Emphasis and Rest. Much delightful Instruction, it is expected, will be derived from this part of the intellectual Feast. Afterwards he will exhibit a Specimen of the projected Edition of the Stratford Swan, which a Retreat from the Stage may perhaps some Time or other (O! may that Time be far distant!) enable him to accomplish. Hence will be introduced an Elucidation of several Passages hitherto totally misunderstood, which will convince Envy herself of the profound Erudition and extensive classical Attainment of Mr. Garrick: it will at the same Time manifest what few are probably apprized of, 'that being the first Actor in the World is far from constituting the most shining and estimable Part of his Character.'

The Whole will conclude with the Apotheosis of Shakespeare.

I am, Sir,

Without Offence to Modesty, I hope,

Smyrna Coffeehouse   A MAN OF LETTERS.[1]
August 19

Both before and after dinner on the first two days musical entertainment was planned at the Great Booth. A general interest in early English songs, ballads, glees, and catches had been aroused by the publication of Bishop Thomas Percy's three-volume collection of *Reliques of Ancient English Poetry* in 1765. Dr Arne, who was a very active member of the Madrigal Club, founded by one of his friends, composed a large number of catches and glees for the meetings of the club, and through his interest this style of composition had become very fashionable.[2] It interested Garrick, as it seemed to him the proper kind of music to have for a

---

[1] *The Public Advertiser*, Aug. 29, 1769, 2, col. 1. The same letter is also printed in *The Gentleman's Magazine*, Aug. 1769, **39**, 375.

[2] Hugh Langley, *Dr Arne*, Cambridge, 1938, 87.

popular festival. So the singing of songs, ballads, catches, and glees, written for the occasion by Garrick, his chief assistant, Isaac Bickerstaffe, and a few others, was planned. Songs were also written for the various processions. All of these had to be set to music. Garrick got into trouble over this; he was a stern taskmaster, often accused of driving hard bargains with those who worked for him. The musicians showed fits of temper and jealousy. Charles Dibdin, the well-known singer and composer, throws interesting light on the tense situation before the Jubilee:

As for my own concern in it, I was a slave to it for months, I set and reset songs to it till my patience was exhausted, which were received or rejected just as ignorance or caprice prevailed . . . yet during all this time, to accommodate him [i.e. Garrick], and indeed for the sake of the cause towards which I had, at least, as sincere good wishes as himself, I bore anything. One thing galled him very much. He really had not an idea of how to write for music, and I frequently ventured at hinting alterations, as to measure, for the advantage of what he wrote. . . . Matters went on in this train, till at last I was so palpably insulted that I declared I would not go to Stratford.[1]

Dibdin had already provided musical settings for *A Warwickshire Lad* and *The Mulberry Tree*, when he heard that Garrick had also asked Aylward and Boyce for settings for those songs and that a private rehearsal of theirs had been given without his presence. However, his settings had been preferred. He nevertheless felt so angry about this slight that he threatened to take all his music away from Garrick; but he finally relented. He continues:

[1] Charles Dibdin, the Elder, *Professional Life of Mr Dibdin*, London, 1803, 1, 78–79.

I had at that time the words of the *Serenade*, '*Let Beauty etc.*' and it was unset. After he [i.e. Garrick] had gone to STRATFORD, I considered that the omission of this very interesting part of the business might not only do material injury to the scheme, but that it might be so represented as to appear a meditated insult to the public. I, therefore, changed my mind, set the words, with accompaniment, as everybody knows, for guitars and flutes, got down to STRATFORD the evening before the *Jubilee*, made the musicians sit up all night, and as it was daylight, we sallied forth as a band of masqueraders, and to the astonishment of Garrick serenaded him with the very thing he had set his heart upon but which he had given up as lost.[1]

Starting on August the 10th, notices were published in the newspapers listing the places where tickets for the Jubilee could be ordered, and finally on August the 31st the following announcement appeared:

NOW READY FOR DELIVERY

Tickets for the Jubilee, at Stratford upon Avon, at one guinea each, at the following places, viz.

The Theatre Royal in Drury Lane; Tom's coffee-house, Russel-street; Mr. Becket's bookseller, in the Strand; Mr. Griffin's bookseller, in Catherine-street; Mr. Jackson's habit shop, in Tavistock-street; Mr Johnson's music shop, York-street; Covent Garden; and at Mr. Peyton's, at the White Lion, in Stratford.

N.B. Tickets for the Masquerade, on Thursday the 7th of September, will be delivered at Stratford upon Avon.[2]

The ticket reproduced below may be seen at the Folger Shakespeare Library (another may be seen at the Shakespeare Museum, Stratford on Avon).

[1] Charles Dibdin, the Elder, *Professional Life of Mr Dibdin*, London, 1803, I, 80.
[2] *The London Evening Post*, Aug. 29, 1769.

D

While all the preparations for the Jubilee were going on, Garrick's numerous enemies, including scholars, commentators, dissatisfied actors, and playwrights, tried their best to belittle and ridicule both the Jubilee and Garrick himself. Outstanding among his enemies at

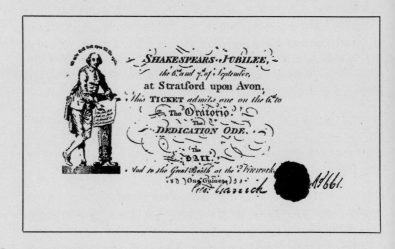

this time were the commentator George Steevens, the author William Kenrick and the actor Samuel Foote. Articles appeared claiming that Warburton or Dr Johnson would have been a more appropriate choice for President of the Jubilee; they also contained vicious attacks on the Mayor and Corporation of Stratford, which caused great annoyance. A letter, signed AVONIENSIS, stated the case of the Corporation. It was published on August the 12th in answer to a letter signed ALETHES that had appeared on July the 29th. The author writes:

... The uncouth Images, the Embarrassment of Words from which the Sentiment is constantly struggling to get free, are such peculiar Characteristics of the Author, that one cannot easily mistake him; and the liberal Abuse he has thrown out against the Corporation of Stratford is the genuine Product of Malice and Dullness; . . . there needs no other Proof than the Letter of Alethes to shew, that the low, scurrilous Stuff that has disgraced your Paper, was dictated by Envy of the most malignant Kind, which like it's ancient Type the *Hydra* has cast forth it's Gall through the various mouths of *Anti-squeezum, Desqueese-oh!! Alethes*, etc., etc., for depend upon it, by the internal Evidence of Composition, they are all different Names for the same Person: and so Sir, we are both Fools and Knaves, because we did not elect Johnson for our President.[1]

The writer then continues with a straight, factual account of the proceedings of the Corporation at the meeting where Garrick was elected president of the Jubilee, showing that the names of Warburton and Johnson had been suggested, but that after due consideration Garrick had been unanimously elected as the most suitable for the post.

Some letter-writers insinuated that both Garrick and the inhabitants of Stratford were chiefly interested in the mercenary aspects of the Jubilee and were ready to exploit and fleece the visitors. Several poems and songs appearing during August stressed this aspect. *Shakespeare's Feast*, an ode, generally thought to be by George Steevens, was published on August the 5th. In form it is an imitation of Dryden's *Alexander's Feast*, and it heaps gross ridicule upon the Stratford mayor and George Keate.[2] On August the 15th the following song appeared in a newspaper:

[1] *The Public Advertiser*, Aug. 12, 1769, 1, col. 4.
[2] Ibid., Aug. 5, 1769, 2, col. 2.

Come brothers of Stratford, these flocks let us shear,
Which bright as if washed in our Avon appear!
The coolest are they who from fleeces are free,
And who are such trimmers, such trimmers as we?
Sing Tantara, shear all etc., etc.

By mode and caprice are these Londoners led,
For dinner they'll pay what we charge 'em a head:
. . .

As soon as they've gone, all our gains we'll reveal,
As light as the flocks we have shear'd, they shall feel:
While we with their money are jolly and gay,
And leave to next year the return of the day.
Sing Tantara, shear all, etc.[1]

Two days later another song appeared in the same newspaper:

A TRIP TO THE JUBILEE

The Wise-men of Avon, by shrewd deputation,
Presented to GARRICK their wooden donation;
   And wished, as I'm told,
   It had been all of gold,
Like those his great Actorship had sometimes since
Of Denmark's young King, and the Parmesan Prince.[2]
   My good Friends, said he,
   It is all one to me,
Tho' the box be cut of a mulberry tree;
   For 'tis just the same thing,
Tho' itself be not gold, if but gold it will bring.

---

[1] *The London Chronicle*, Aug. 15–17, 1769, **26**, 160, 1.

[2] Ibid., Aug. 15–17, 1769, **26**, 160, 1–2. Both had recently visited England. The young Danish King, Christian VII, ascended the throne in 1766. He married Caroline Mathilda, a sister of George III. His behaviour in England was eccentric and he later became insane. The Parmesan Prince was of the House of Bourbon-Parma that had come into power in 1748.

The Philosopher's Stone,
It is very well known,
Is a Genius, like mine,
That can carve, clip and coin.
Or like to King Midas convert, at a touch,
Wood or gold, or, what's better, turn little to much:
Hence, so long as the world's full of nifeys and ninneys,[1]
My mulberry-box will be full of good guineas.

The Mayor of Old Stratford, in strange agitation,
T'have miss'd being 'prentic'd to such a vocation,
Replied, would your Actorship teach us the way,
We are apt, and don't doubt that our parts we could play;
   This present of wood
   Shews our hearts to be good:
   But if once we are told
   How to turn it to gold,
The trunks of our tree we would bring on our backs,
Lop the boughs, stack the roots, and you still should go snacks.
   Enough, Friends, says he.
   Bring the mulberry tree.
And I will ensure you a fine Jubilee.
'A Jubilee! Gemini! George! what is that?'
No questions, I know, my good friends, what I'm at:
Make me, but your JUBILEE-DAVY, my trick is
To turn all the world into JUBILEE-DICKIES.*

M. H.[2]

* See Farquhar's *Constant Couple.*

This newspaper feud between Garrick's enemies and his friends produced an endless number of grossly abusive articles, fables, parodies, and poems. Horace

---

[1] *nifeys,* probably a variant of the Scotch dialect word *niffy,* which appears only as an adjective in *O.E.D.*

[2] *The London Chronicle,* Aug. 15–17, 1769, 26, 160, 1–2.

Walpole, who was in Paris during the Jubilee, was thoroughly disgusted with the whole business. Upon his return to England he wrote to his friend George Montagu on October the 16th:

I have blushed at Paris when the papers came over crammed with ribaldry, or with Garrick's insufferable nonsense about Shakespeare. As that man's writings will be preserved by his name, who will believe that he was a tolerable actor? . . . Garrick's prologues and epilogues are as bad as his pindarics and pantomimes.[1]

The feud in the papers kept the coming jubilee before the public, and as a matter of fact was excellent publicity for the festival. Garrick's friends would naturally want to attend it, and his enemies could not resist the temptation to go down to Stratford to see Garrick make a fool of himself. But William Kenrick apparently did not want to come, for on August the 24th the following poem was published in a newspaper:

For the Public Advertiser

An EPISTLE *to Mr.* KENRICK, *on his declining to accept an Invitation* to Stratford upon Avon.*

> How, Mr. *Kenrick,* is it true
> That you, of all the World, shou'd, you!
> Of *Shakespeare* be neglectful?
> Not to the *Jubilee* come down,
> 'Gainst Sept. the 6th, to *Stratford* Town!
> How monstrous disrespectful!

---

* Written in Imitation of Mr. K's Epistle to D. Garrick, Esq.; on his Return from Italy.

[1] Walpole, op. cit., 10, 298.

We thought that you, to whom the Bard
Had shewn that singular Regard,
    To none e'er shewn before ye,
That you, in whom he deign'd t'inspire
A Spark of his own Muse of Fire,
    Shou'd burn for Shakespeare's Glory.

In vain we chuckled, in the Pit,
At *Falstaff's Wedding*,* to his Wit,
    For Shakespeare's Fame solicitous:
If he, who must his Ghost have seen,
Determines, out of Pride or Spleen,
    At Stratford not to visit us.

In vain 'mong Princes, Poets, Peers,
May *Garrick* beat up Volunteers,
    His spouse attend the Ladies:
In vain by *George* and *Latimore*,
And Doctor *Arne*, so long before,
    Such preparations made is.

In vain may *Johnson*, *Capel*, *Keate*,
See, envious, to the Steward's Seat
    The little Man exalted;
Painful Pre-eminence, to sit,
And feed the gaping Crowd with Wit,
    Unless 'tis highly salted!

. . .

Dreadfully dull will be their Greeting
At this intended merry Meeting,
    If, heedless in the Tomb,
Great Shakespeare hide his sleeping Head,
Sit sullen with the silent Dead,
    Or chat with John a Coomb.†

* A comedy so called, written by Mr. K. in Imitation of Shakespeare.
† A famous Miser, on whom Shakespeare made an Epitaph.

What will avail on Stratford's Stones
To shake our Trotters o'er his Bones,
    Unless we raise his Sprite?
Come, then, and with thee bring the Charm,
That Death and Dullness can disarm,
    The Laughter-loving Knight.*

The soul of Shakespeare then shall rise,
And, Pleasure sparkling in his Eyes,
    Inspire the joyous Mummery;
Else will the Whole be horrid, low,
A very Flockton's Puppet-Show,
    Damn'd, vile, insipid Flummery!

J.B. [1]

Stratford, Aug. 17,

* Sir John Falstaff.[1]

The writer of these verses, who signed himself J.B.,
was certainly not James Boswell, who at that time was
still at Edinburgh and had shown no particular interest
in the jubilee. Kenrick, however, changed his mind and
did go to Stratford after all. So did Garrick's other
enemy, Samuel Foote from the Haymarket Theatre,
widely feared for his habit of inserting topical allusions
and caricatures of his contemporaries into his parts.
Garrick, whose vanity was easily hurt, was seriously
afraid of his sharp wit and tongue. There were rumours
that Foote would stay in London:

It has been strongly reported here, that the modern Aristophanes
intends to entertain his audience during the Jubilee, with a *mock
one* at his own theatre, which in the opinion of some, will exceed
our own; as *Mock-Turtle* is grateful to many of those palates
which have no relish for the true one.[2]

[1] *The Public Advertiser*, Aug. 24, 1769, 2, col. 2.
[2] *Lloyd's Evening Post*, Sept. 1-4, 1769, 25, 219, 2.

Weeks before the actual jubilee, crowds gathered in Stratford, coming from London, from the neighbourhood of Stratford, and from the adjoining counties.

Great numbers of the nobility and gentry arrived a week or ten days before the appointed time to secure their lodgings against the approaching meeting; and Stratford, as well as towns and villages in the neighbourhood, was completely filled, previous to its commencement, by those, whose zeal prompted them to be present at this high festival.[1]

Samuel Foote's biographer, William Cooke, makes the following comment:

The Jubilee . . . met the approbation not only of the *literati*, but of the public at large, as no sooner was the time fixed for its celebration, than everyone within a hundred miles of the place, who was not prevented by pressing circumstances, prepared for attending this august and classical fête. All summer journeys to friends, all trips to watering places were for a while suspended; while 'Avon's banks where flowers eternal blow', formed the great resort of all.[2]

As early as September the 2nd a visitor wrote:

At Peyton's . . . there were upwards of forty carriages, and at night they were obliged to turn several great families away. . . . A Londoner, who came to town this morning . . . assures us that all the inns and roads from London are filled, as if an army was upon its march.[3]

Ten London mercers from the neighbourhood of Covent Garden showed ingenuity about the trip to Stratford:

---

[1] Wheler, op. cit., 169.
[2] William Cooke, *Memoirs of Samuel Foote*, Esq., London, 1805, I, 164.
[3] *The London Chronicle*, Sept. 5–7, 1769, 26, 238, 1.

They hired a large, broad wheel waggon, in which they slung several cots or hammocks and occasionally took spell and spell; they stored it with all kinds of provisions, wine, etc., tables and chairs, which served them as the song says, 'for parlour, for kitchen, for hall', by which means they travelled with great convenience, little fatigue and moderate expence, having always their commodious carriage to retire to, without being liable to the general complaint of the want of bed, board and lodging, at the same time that they were defended from the heat of the weather in their excursions, as well as from the violent rains that followed.[1]

A new means of transportation, Mr Moore's recent invention of a so-called 'horseless carriage', was much discussed at this time. Pictures show it to have been shaped like a carriage, not drawn by horses but propelled by foot-power applied to pedals. On August the 13th the following announcement appeared, which almost certainly is facetious:

For Lloyd's Evening Post

A CARD

Miss Lucy Cooper presents her compliments to Mr. Moore, and begs the favour of him, as she is going to set up her carriage, to let her know at what time his Machine will be absolutely ready to perform, as she is very desirous of purchasing one for her expedition to Shakespeare's Jubilee; and, from the number of disappointments the Public have met with upon this occasion, begins to fear, that Mr. Moore's Invention will turn out like several other *Machines* that went without horses, which she has formerly made *trial* of but which never turned out, in any respect, to her *satisfaction*.[2]

It looks, however, as if Garrick had hoped to make use of such 'horseless carriages' from the following 'intelligence' from Stratford dated August the 29th:

[1] *The London Evening Post*, Sept. 16, 1769.
[2] *Lloyd's Evening Post*, Aug. 11–14, 1769, **25**, 151.

Those who are to be employed in the decorations of the Hall, etc. are brought down as fast as room can be found for them in the waggons, stages, etc.

N.B. The failure of Mr. Moore's machine has occasioned much unlooked for expence to the Managers in the article of carriage.[1]

On August the 31st the musicians set out for Stratford:

At four o'clock on Sunday morning the Gentlemen of the Band of Music, who are to perform in Stratford upon Avon, set out, in grand Cavalcade, from Mr. Pritchard's, in Oxford Road; there were ten coaches and four, six post-chaises, and a great number of saddle-horses.[2]

On the same day the Garricks and the Angelos started their journey to Stratford in their own coaches. The Garricks had invited the Angelos to pass the evening with them at Oxford. They had an uneventful trip to Oxford, but Mr Angelo, who had started at 6 a.m., ran into some trouble. His son writes:

He had intended to take post horses on the road at a certain distance from London; but he had certainly 'reckoned without his host', for every beast of burden had been engaged, at every inn, for several days before; hence his own horses were obliged to go through the journey, which distressed the poor animals, and made our arrival at Oxford later than was intended; we did not get thither until near eight. Our friends were fearful that some accident had delayed us.[3]

Young Henry Angelo remembered that Mr Garrick had brought some very fine fruit from Hampton House for their dessert and that they all spent a very pleasant evening. The Garricks left early the next morning for Stratford. They had with them Benjamin Wilson, the

[1] *Lloyd's Evening Post*, Sept. 1–4, 1769, **25**, 219, 2.
[2] Ibid., Sept. 4–6, 1769, **25**, 226, 3.
[3] Angelo, op. cit., **1**, 42.

distinguished portrait painter. The Angelos left somewhat later to give their horses time to recover their
strength, as one of them was in rather bad condition.
There was still no chance of hiring other horses, but the
Master of the Star Inn told Angelo that he knew a pair
of carriage-horses worth his notice that could be bought
for the small sum of thirty-two guineas. Angelo bought
them on the spot.[1] Garrick had acquired comfortable
lodgings for the Angelos at a grocer's in the market-
place; the Garricks were staying at the house of Mr
Hunt, the town clerk, where Boswell later called on them.
Garrick also furnished food for the Angelos' table. They
considered themselves very fortunate 'as hundreds of
persons of consideration, among the multitudes who
filled the town, could procure no accommodations, even
at any price'.[2]

Cradock and his group arrived the day before the
Jubilee. They brought cold provisions with them and
deposited them at a baker's house, as had been arranged beforehand. Cradock gives the following details:

> We first wished, however, to drive to the great inn, but arriving
> in the neighbouring street, we found that there were so many
> loose horses, that the ladies could not safely alight, till Mr. Peyton
> privately conveyed them by another route to his house, and placed
> them in security in Mrs. Peyton's bed-chamber, till our supper
> could be served up on the landing-place of the great stairs.[3]

Many letters to the newspapers describe the excitement
felt in Stratford in the days just before the opening of the
jubilee, supplying many details, as the following:

---

[1] Angelo, I, 50. Angelo commits the error of calling the painter Robert
Wilson.

[2] Ibid., I, 43-44.

[3] Cradock, op. cit., I, 215.

There are great numbers of people every night diverting themselves on and near the water, playing off fireworks, which they
purchase of the workmen belonging to that part, they having
completed their principal intention; and it is a most pleasing sight
to look at them as they now stand in the order they are to be
played off.[1]

Another visitor writes that on Wednesday night
'Seigneur Angelo is to conclude with his Pots de Feu,
Vertical Wheels, Tourbillions, Air Balloons, Line
Rockets, and the whole Machinery of Pyrotechny'.[2] The
first letter continues:

We have about 30 very small brass pieces, 12 cohorns and some
mortars, which are kept almost continually firing to divert the
company; which for quantity, to those who do not see it every day,
would appear incredible. . . . As to running horses, I think there
are six in town; however I saw four this morning, and people
offer wagers that there will be fourteen. — Wenches! never was
any paradise so plentifully or beautifully inhabited as at this time.
. . . Here are people of all trades and professions, with goods to
dispose of, from all parts of the kingdom; so that if a person has but
money, he cannot stand in need of any articles his desires may demand of him.[3]

The second letter-writer ends on a wildly enthusiastic
note:

In short, all is Joy and Festivity here, and what with the Rattling
of Coaches, the Blazing and Cracking of Fireworks, the Number
of People going and coming from the Mask Warehouse, whither
they repair to provide themselves with Dresses, my Head is almost
turned and I think I may venture to say I shall never see such
another Scene in all my Life.

[1] *Lloyd's Evening Post*, Sept. 4–6, 1769, **25**, 231, 2.
[2] *The St James Chronicle*, Sept. 5–7, 1769, 4, cols. 3–4.
[3] *Lloyd's Evening Post*, Sept. 4–6, 1769, **25**, 231, 2.

He also speaks about the great crowds:

Every Inn, House and Hovel, now swarms with Company; and the very Stables are no longer confined to the Reception of Horses, or even Grooms and Postillions, the Haylofts over them being cleared for the Reception of Families of the first Credit, who, for Want of better Accommodations are obliged to take up their Lodgings there. The Multitude of Persons brought down by the Manager, in his great Disposition to oblige the Public, by omitting nothing that could contribute to their Entertainment, has not a little helped to fill the Place.

The writer here gives a full list of all the known singers, actresses and musicians that —

are now arrived with an incredible number of Flutes, Hautboys, Fiddlers, Guitars, Candle Snuffers, Scene Shifters, and a numerous Tribe of Attendance from both the Theatres. . . . Among the Gentlemen of Genius and Learning arrived here are Mr. Colman, Mr. Foot, Mr. Bickerstaffe and most others who have ever distinguished themselves by their Talents or Taste for theatrical Writings.[1]

A well-known visitor, who arrived too late for the opening, was James Boswell, who cut a prominent figure at the Jubilee. He had originally made up his mind not to go to Stratford. His engagement to Miss Margaret Montgomerie had been announced late in July, and their marriage was planned for November. We learn from his Journal that he arrived in London from Scotland on September the 1st to put himself under the care of an old physician, Dr Gilbert Kennedy, who dispensed a well-advertised nostrum for venereal disease. He went at once to call on his friend Dr Johnson, but found to his disappointment that he was at Brighton with the Thrales. Miss Williams, the blind poetess, re-

[1] *The St James Chronicle*, Sept. 5–7, 1769, 4, cols. 3–4.

ceived him and urged him to go to the Jubilee. On the
spur of the moment he decided that he would go, if the
doctor, whom he was to see the next day, Saturday,
would consent to postpone his treatment.[1] He writes in
high spirits:

He allowed me to go to Shakespeare's Jubilee before I began my
course of his medicine. I then went to a Mr. Dalemaine, an em-
broiderer in Bow Street, Covent Garden; gave him, cut out in paper
as well as I could, the form of a Corsican cap, and ordered *Viva
la Liberta* to be embroidered on the front of it in letters of gold.[2]

On Monday he searched all over the town for things
needed for his costume as a Corsican chief. He had
acquired such a costume when he was in Corsica, but
had left it in Edinburgh. Of his search for parts for the
costume he writes:

Some I had made on purpose. Others I borrowed. But at last I
got everything in order, and everything I wanted went into such
small bounds that I could carry the whole in my travelling-bag,
except my musket and staff. I met by chance with a most curious
staff in a shop in Cheapside: a very handsome vine with the root
uppermost, and upon it a bird, very well carved. I paid six shillings
for it. After I had bought it, I told the master of the shop, 'Why
this vine is worth any money. It is a Jubilee staff. That bird is the
bird of Avon.'[3]

He started his journey at 7 a.m. the next morning by
taking the stage-coach to Oxford, where he arrived about
6 p.m. He intended to travel part of the way to Stratford
that night, so as to reach the town in time for the opening
of the Jubilee, but he found pleasant company at the inn
in Oxford and also decided to write a letter to his beloved Margaret, so that it was near midnight when he

[1] *The Private Papers of James Boswell,* 6, *Boswell in Search of a Wife.* Edited
by Frank Brady and Frederick A. Pottle, New York, 1956, 269.
[2] Ibid., 271.   [3] Ibid., 274.

set out in a post-chaise alone for Stratford. He was nervous, afraid of being robbed, and therefore hid his watch, his purse, and his pocket-book in different pockets in the chaise. He had to change into another vehicle at Woodstock, and then suddenly discovered, after he had driven a considerable distance, that he had forgotten his pocket-book with several important papers in it in the first chaise. This meant that he would have to go back to Woodstock and possibly to Oxford to retrieve the pocket-book. He describes this situation very vividly:

When I arrived at Woodstock, the landlord had my pocket-book for me. I was comforted and happy. I took breakfast, it being near six in the morning. But I was now in a new difficulty. Such crowds had passed that there was no post-chaise to be had. Here then was I, on the very morning of the Jubilee, in danger of not getting to it in time. I became very impatient, so hired a couple of horses and off I set, the postillion carrying part of my baggage and myself the rest. I had no boots, and only a short greatcoat which I had borrowed of a postillion, and it rained pretty thick. I was really distressed, and the fear that my health would suffer made me worse. However, at the end of six miles, I found a post-chaise into which I got directly, and partly by threatenings, partly by promises, prevailed on the post-boys to drive fast, and arrived at Stratford between twelve and one.[1]

He went to the White Lion Inn, which of course was full, but from there he was shown to 'a tolerable old-fashioned room with a neat, clean bed'.[2] The price was a guinea a night. The room was near by, opposite Shakespeare's birthplace. It seems strange that he had no difficulty in finding accommodation at a reasonable price, although he arrived after the Jubilee had begun.

[1] James Boswell, *The Private Papers of James Boswell*, 6, *Boswell in Search of a Wife*, Edited by Frank Brady and Frederick A. Pottle, New York, 1956, 279–80.   [2] *Ibid.*, 280.

II

Description of the Jubilee

At six o'clock in the morning the festival was opened
with the ringing of bells and 'a triple discharge of seventeen pieces of cannon and twelve mortars, planted on the
banks of the Avon'.[1] It must have aroused all the visitors
at Stratford and in the vicinity, but whether they ap-
preciated such an early awakening remains unknown.
As soon as the cannonade was over, the musicians and
singers from the Drury Lane Theatre, who were disguised as waits with their faces smeared with dirt, 'sallied
forth as a band of masqueraders'[2] with guitars and flutes
to serenade Garrick and the principal lady visitors with
the following song:

The MORNING ADDRESS

To the Ladies

LET beauty with the sun arise,
    To SHAKESPEARE tribute pay,
With heavenly smiles and speaking eyes,
    Give grace and lustre to the day.

[1] *The Universal Magazine*, Sept. 1759, 45, 158.
[2] Dibdin, op. cit., 1, 80.

Each smile she gives protects his name,
What face shall dare to frown?
Not Envy's self can blast the fame
Which Beauty deigns to crown.[1]

As mentioned before, Garrick, who had written the text, was pleasantly surprised, for he had had reason to believe that Dibdin would not set it to music in time for the opening. After serenading the ladies the band marched through the streets singing several new ballads, among them *Warwickshire*, likewise with words by Garrick and music by Dibdin. It caught on immediately and became a favourite with the crowds. It had seven stanzas, of which the fourth and the fifth give a vivid impression of the nature of the ballad:

Old Ben, Thomas Otway, John Dryden,
And half a score more we take pride in,
Of famous *Will Congreve,* we boast too the skill,
But the *Will* of all *Wills,* was *Warwickshire Will*
Warwickshire Will,
Matchless still,
For the *Will* of all *Wills,* was a *Warwickshire Will.*

Our SHAKESPEARE compar'd is to no man,
Nor *Frenchman,* nor *Grecian,* nor *Roman,*
Their swans are all geese, to the *Avon's* sweet swan,
And the man of all men, was a *Warwickshire* man,
Warwickshire man,
Avon's swan
And the man of all men, was a *Warwickshire* man.[2]

---

[1] *Shakespeare's Garland* Being a collection of new songs, ballads, roundelays, catches, glees, comic-serenatas, etc., performed at the jubilee at Stratford upon Avon. The music by Dr Arne, Mr Barthelemon, Mr Ailwood, and Mr Dibdin. London, 1769, p. 1.
[2] Ibid., 2–4.

Printed handbills were left at every house to inform the
visitors about the entertainments planned for the day and
the night.[1] There was to be a public breakfast at the Town
Hall at nine o'clock. To this every holder of a guinea
ticket to the Jubilee would be admitted upon the payment of a shilling. Garrick arrived at the Town Hall a
little after eight o'clock to see that everything was
properly prepared and to be ready to receive the company. At the same time the newly elected mayor, John
Meacham, and the corporation 'in their formalities' met
in the Old Guild Hall and, led by the mayor, went in
procession through the streets to the ballroom of the
new Town Hall to wait on Garrick, before the public
breakfast began. A brief ceremony was held, at which
William Hunt, the town clerk, delivered the following
address:

Sir, You, who have done the memory of Shakespeare so much
honour, are esteemed to be the fittest person to be appointed the
first steward of this jubilee; which we beg your acceptance of:
permit me, Sir, in obedience to the commands of the corporation,
to deliver to you this medal and this wand, the sacred pledges of
our veneration for our immortal townsman, whereby you are
invested with your office.[2]

Both the wand and the large medal were made of wood
from the famous mulberry tree. On the medal was a carving of the bust of Shakespeare, richly set in gold (see
illustration facing p. 63). Garrick made a gracious speech
of acceptance, fastened the medal round his neck, and
wore it throughout the jubilee. The end of this ceremony
was indicated by another ringing of bells and firing of
cannon.

[1] Victor, op. cit., 3, 209.   [2] Wheler, op. cit., 170–1.

After this the ballroom, which would hold about eight hundred people, was quickly filled by the breakfast crowd. Tea, coffee and chocolate were served. The note on the distributed handbills urging the visitors to buy and wear the special Shakespeare favours, i.e. the medals and the rainbow-coloured ribbons, had been effective. 'Ribbon favours were universally worn by the ladies as well as the gentlemen, from the most elevated rank, to persons of the meanest situations: the silver medals . . . were also worn by vast numbers present and had a very handsome appearance.'[1] Among the members of the nobility present were 'The Duke of Dorset, Lord Beauchamp, Lord Grosvenor, Lord Archer . . . Lord Denbigh, Lord Spencer and Lord Craven'.[2] The drums and fifes of the Warwickshire militia, in their new uniforms, played opposite the Town Hall to entertain the company and gave great satisfaction. Breakfast must also have been served at the Great Booth, for correspondents to three London newspapers[3] mentioned that they had breakfast there and were likewise entertained by a band, so that it looks as if the overflow crowd went there. The Great Booth and the new Town Hall were so different in appearance that it would seem impossible to make a mistake about the building.

An important part of Garrick's plan for the jubilee was that the public should march from one entertainment to the next in an orderly procession led by a band, as had been the custom at early English folk festivals. So when breakfast was over such a procession started from the Town Hall (and apparently another from the Great

[1] Wheler, op. cit., 172.
[2] *The Universal Magazine*, Sept. 1769, 45, 158–9.
[3] *The Morning Chronicle, The London Evening Post, Lloyd's Evening Post.*

Commemorative Handkerchief

(in the possession of the Shakespeare Birthplace Trust: believed to be the only example
in existence)

The Scene at the High Cross

(Contemporary water-colour in the possession of the Shakespeare Birthplace Trust)

Booth) at 10.30 a.m. to reach the Great Collegiate
Church in time for the next entertainment, viz. the performance of Dr Arne's oratorio *Judith* (book by Isaac
Bickerstaffe), with Dr Arne himself as the conductor.[1] It
was scheduled to begin at eleven o'clock. A large temporary orchestra had been erected under the organ to
hold the singers and the whole Drury Lane band. The
singers were Mrs Baddeley; Mrs Barthelemon, Dr
Arne's niece; Miss Weller, Dr Arne's pupil; Mr Vernon; Mr Champness and Master Brown. 'At the end of
the first act Mr. Barthelemon played a most enchanting solo, on the violin'.[2] Most accounts agree that the
band was excellent, the airs well-performed, the choruses
very full and that the performance gave great satisfaction
and was well attended, but there were some dissenting
voices.

A modern reader cannot but wonder how Garrick
justified the use of the oratorio for the opening entertainment at the jubilee. Its only connection with Shakespeare was the fact that it was performed in the church
where he lies buried, but its lofty solemnity was supposed to lend an air of dignity to the festival. Cradock,
seriously questioning the appropriateness of the oratorio
for the occasion, makes the following comment:

. . . the airs were all given in the best style, but the chorusses were
almost as meagre as the appearance of the audience; and I felt
much hurt for all that were engaged to perform in it. The company of any rank had not half arrived; and an Oratorio was but a
cold introduction to a tumultuous Jubilee.[3]

[1] 'Judith', highly praised by Dibdin, had been performed at the Drury
Lane Theatre in February 1761 and repeated twice in March 1761 and
again at Lent 1762 (Langley, op. cit., 89).

[2] Wheler, op. cit., 172.   [3] Cradock, op. cit., I, 215–16.

Dibdin, who was an extravagant admirer of Dr Arne's work but disliked Garrick on account of his capriciousness and well-known stinginess, was highly critical about the jubilee. At a much later date he wrote:

Certainly there was a large assemblage of elegance and fashion at STRATFORD, and every person came there determined to be happy. . . . At a jubilee it was a strange thing to introduce an oratorio, and though it was *Judith*, one of the most noble compositions that ever stampt fame on a musician, its beauties were not felt. I cannot give a better idea of this business than extracting some particulars from an elaborate panegyric on this celebrated subject, by the good-natured JEMMY BOSWELL, who was hired, not by money, but by well-timed flattery, to praise it.[1]

He is here thinking not only of the oratorio but of the jubilee in general. His accusation against Boswell was obviously unjust, for Boswell was honestly enthusiastic about the festival, as he shows in his letter to *The Public Advertiser* written after his return to London and published on September the 16th. For very obvious reasons he barely mentions the oratorio, saying that 'it was an admirable performance', but he adds a typical Boswellian emotional remark:

. . . I could have wished, that Prayers had been read, and a short Sermon preached. It would have consecrated our Jubilee, to begin it with Devotion, with gratefully adoring the Supreme Father of all Spirits from whom cometh every good and perfect Gift.[2]

The reason why he said so little about the oratorio was simply that he arrived too late to hear much, if any, of it. The oratorio had started at eleven o'clock, but Boswell did not reach Stratford till between twelve and one and had to find a room before he could go to the church. He seems

---

[1] Dibdin, op. cit., 1, 75.
[2] *The Public Advertiser*, Sept. 16, 1769, 2. col. 1.

to have arrived just as the performance was over and the people were beginning to leave. His account of this in his *Journal* is vivid and utterly characteristic of him:

Having fixed this point [i.e. of getting a room], I went immediately to the great church. It was surrounded by a crowd of people; and, as objects anyhow similar call up similar circumstances, I could not help thinking of the Monday's meeting after giving the sacrament in a country church in Scotland. I was exceedingly dirty; my hair hung wet about my ears; my black suit and the postillion's grey duffle above it, several inches too short every way, made a very strange appearance. I could observe people getting together and whispering about me, for the church was full of well-dressed people. At last Mr. Garrick observed me. We first made an attitude to each other and then cordially shook hands. I gave him a line I had written to let him know I was incognito, as I wished to appear in the Corsican dress for the first time they should know me. Many of those who had stared, seeing that I was intimate with the steward of the Jubilee, came up and asked who I was. He answered, 'A clergyman in disguise.' To see a noble band of the first musicians from London with Dr. Arne at their head, Mr. Garrick, a number of nobility and gentry and of the learned and ingenious assembled to do honour to Shakespeare in his native place, gave me much satisfaction.[1]

When the oratorio was finished, Garrick, with the medal round his neck and the wand in his hand, walked from the church at the head of the procession of the band and the performers who 'to the accompaniment of the proper instruments' sang the following chorus:

> This is the day, a holiday! a holiday!
> Drive spleen and rancour far away,
> This is the day, a holiday! a holiday!
> Drive care and sorrow far away.[2]

[1] *Boswell in Search of a Wife*, 280–1.
[2] *Shakespeare's Garland*, 14.

Many visitors joined the procession on foot, but it was also 'attended by a large cavalcade of the nobility and gentry, in their coaches, chaises, etc.'[1] The procession stopped at the birthplace, where the chorus continued with the following stanza:

> Here Nature nurs'd her darling boy,
>   From whom all care and sorrow fly,
>   Whose harp the muses strung:
>   From heart to heart let joy rebound,
>   Now, now, we tread enchanted ground,
>   Here SHAKESPEARE walk'd, and sung![2]

The birthplace (see illustration, p. 2) became a major attraction to the public. After the jubilee a newspaper correspondent, signing himself 'A Friend to true Merit', made the following comment:

It is scarce credible the Number of Persons of all Ranks that came to see it, and the Enthusiasm of some was very remarkable! The Joy and the Satisfaction which they felt at being in the very Room in which the great Man was born exceeds all Description. It was not confined to the English only, for the Scotch and the Irish were as eager in paying their devotion.[3]

At the birthplace Thomas Becket, the official publisher to the jubilee, had set up his shop in a ground-floor room, believed to be the birth room, and here among other items *Shakespeare's Garland*, the official collection of songs and ballads, etc., written for the occasion, as well as Garrick's *Ode*, to be performed the next day, and *Shakespeare's Jubilee*, *A Masque* by George Saville Carey, were for sale.

---

[1] Wheler, op. cit., 172.
[2] *Shakespeare's Garland*, 14.
[3] *The Public Advertiser*, Sept. 16, 1769, 3, col. 1.

From the birthplace the procession marched on to the Amphitheatre or the Great Booth. The company was most favourably impressed with the big room and its beautiful decorations. It admired the gilded bases and capitals of the eight painted columns that supported the roof. Boswell writes that 'between the Pillars were Crimson Curtains, very well imitated, as hanging over each Recess. In this Amphitheatre was a large Orchestra placed as it used to be formerly at Ranelagh.'[1] This was large enough to hold more than fifty musicians and singers, in rows raised one above the other (see illustration, p. 70).

At three o'clock a public ordinary, priced at 10*s.* 6*d.* including the wine, was served with Garrick presiding as steward. This was an elegant and sumptuous meal 'including all the rarities the season could afford'. It was exceedingly well attended; Victor, the theatre historian, estimated the people present at about seven hundred, others thought that more than one thousand participated in the meal. The diners were pleased with the food and the wine, but a few thought that the service was too slow. One visitor states that he 'drank both claret and madeira, both good'. He continues:

After dinner lord Grosvenor proposed a bumper to the steward – and Mr. Garrick, (whose behaviour exhibited the greatest politeness, with the truest liveliness and hilarity) another to the memory of the Bard, to which was subjoined three cheers, at the instance of your humble servant, most heartily. The performers in the orchestra then began the catches and glees, which were absolutely inspiring and the company joined in the chorus.[2]

[1] *The Public Advertiser*, Sept. 16, 1769, 2, col. 1.
[2] *The Gentleman's Magazine*, Sept. 1769, 39, 422.

Garrick had written the words for a number of these pieces, in fact for all the most popular ones, such as 'Warwickshire', 'The Mulberry Tree', and 'Sweet Willy-O'. Dr Arne, Dibdin, and the other Drury Lane musicians had provided the tunes. Obviously this entertainment, with

The Loving Cup

the audience joining in the singing, was a great success. The Mayor and Corporation now presented Garrick with a loving cup, made of wood from the mulberry tree and lined with gold. It was set in a tall silver stand. [This cup is now the property of the Folger Shakespeare

Library and is on exhibition there.]¹ Garrick was prepared for the event. Although Dibdin always insisted
that Garrick could not sing, he raised the cup in his hand
and sang the ballad of 'Shakespeare's Mulberry-Tree',
which he had written for the occasion. The ballad has
eight stanzas, each of four lines with a long refrain. The
most characteristic of these are the following:

1. BEHOLD this fair goblet, 'twas carv'd from the tree,
   Which, O my sweet SHAKESPEARE, was planted by thee;
   As a relick I kiss it, and bow at the shrine,
   What comes from thy hand must be ever divine!
       All shall yield to the Mulberry-tree,
           Bend to thee,
           Blest Mulberry,
           Matchless was he
           Who planted thee,
       And thou like him immortal be!

· · · · · ·

6. The fame of the patron gives fame to the tree,
   From him and his merits this takes its degree;
   Let *Phoebus* and *Bacchus* their glories resign,
   Our tree shall surpass both the Laurel and Vine
       All shall yield to the Mulberry-tree,
           etc., etc.

· · · · · ·

8. Then each take a relick of this hallow'd tree,
   From folly and fashion a charm let it be;
   Fill fill to the planter, the cup to the brim,
   To honour the country, do honour to him.
       All shall yield to the Mulberry-tree,
           etc., etc.²

¹ *Collectanea*, 2, 107. The Folger Shakespeare Library.
² *Shakespeare's Garland*, 7–9.

Boswell was enthusiastic about the song; he found 'Sweet Willy-O' tender and pathetic and the chorus of 'The Mulberry-Tree' very fine, but he praised 'Warwickshire' most highly as:

a Ballad of great Merit in it's Kind, lively, spirited, full of witty Turns and even delicate Fancies. Mr. Garrick's Words and Mr. Dibdin's Music, went charmingly together and we all joined in the Chorus.[1]

Several visitors commented on the feeling of harmony and fellowship that prevailed. About six o'clock the entertainment closed with the performers and the audience singing 'God Save the King'. 'A Friend of true Merit', quoted above, reports in his letter:

After the Songs, Catches, and Glees were sung, the Cup or Goblet made of the Mulberry Tree, and lined with Gold, was seized by the Company, and nothing would satisfy them till it was filled with the best of Wines, that they might have the pleasure to drink to the Memory of the immortal Bard. – The Cup went around very freely indeed, and the enthusiastic Joy upon the Occasion was very remarkable!

He continues his report with an amusing incident which happened to the custodian of the cup on his way home from the Amphitheatre when he was surrounded by friends,

who earnestly requested . . . the Pleasure of drinking some . . . Shakespeare Ale out of the Cup. As it was a Time of Mirth and Jollity, there was no refusing them; the Ale was called for, the Cup was filled, and every one did Honour to it. The Company soon increased, and every Lad and Lass, as well as every Darby

---

[1] *The Public Advertiser*, Sept. 16, 1769, 2, col. 1.

Mr Garrick

as Steward of the Stratford Jubilee September 1769

Garrick as Steward

(Engraving by T. Saunders from the painting by Benjamin van der Gucht)

The Jubilee Medal

Garrick's Medallion
(both in the possession of the
Shakespeare Birthplace Trust)

and Joan, were permitted to partake of the Jollity. One among us, remarkable for his Talent of Singing, with his usual Good-nature gave us *The Warwickshire Lad* and *The Mulberry Tree*; it made the Young and the Old caper about the Room . . . I have been at many a Merrymaking, but must own I never saw the like before. We restored the Cup, with three Cheers for the divine Bard, and three more to his truest Representative Mr. Garrick, and then departed with that Satisfaction such a heart-felt Scene could inspire.[1]

After the entertainment tea and coffee were served at the Amphitheatre. Boswell, having met a number of friends and acquaintances, was in a gay group for the dinner and almost lost his heart to a lively Irish lady, but recovered himself nobly by thinking hard of his lovely fiancée, Margaret Montgomerie. He mentions that he had tea with David Ross, actor and manager of the Edinburgh Theatre, and his wife the celebrated Fanny Murray; Ross introduced him to Thomas King, the comedian, and Mrs King. Boswell found King 'a genteel, agreeable man'.[2] About seven o'clock all the visitors went home to their lodgings to prepare for the evening assembly ball at nine o'clock. Victor noticed that during the interval:

a great Number of Hands were employed to decorate and illuminate the AMPHITHEATRE. When Night approached, the Inhabitants of Stratford testified their Joy by lighting up every Window in every House . . . in every Street in the Town. This made the Night as cheerful as the Day.[3]

All the beautiful painted silk transparencies, at the Town Hall, at the Birthplace and on the bank of the river

[1] *The Public Advertiser*, Sept. 16, 1769, 3, col. 1.
[2] *Boswell in Search of a Wife*, 282.
[3] Victor, op. cit., 3, 213–14.

opposite the Amphitheatre, were illuminated and much admired. For Boswell's enthusiastic description of them, see p. 18.

The Assembly Ball started between nine and ten o'clock in the Amphitheatre, which was brilliantly illuminated by a huge chandelier. The hall was crowded with company; many members of nobility and gentry were present, among them 'The Duke of Manchester, Lord Northampton, Lord Hertford, Lord Carlisle, Lord Shrewsbury, Lord Pigot etc.'[1] Boswell, exhausted from travelling all through the preceding night, writes in his Journal:

I went to the ball tonight, just to see how the company looked when dressed, and to be able to tell that I had been there. I was so sleepy that I could hardly stand upon my feet, so I went home and went to bed immediately. My landlady got me warm negus, and seemed to be a good motherly woman. I told her that perhaps I might retire from the world and just come and live in my room at Stratford.[2]

At the Assembly minuets were danced till midnight, when country dances began and continued till three o'clock in the morning. One of the guests found that the ball was 'remarkable chiefly for the most elegant minuet I ever saw or ever shall see, danced by Mrs. G.— and Mr.—'[3] This is not surprising, since Mrs Garrick had been a well-known ballet dancer before her marriage. To

---

[1] *The London Chronicle*, Sept. 7–9, 1769, 26, 248, 1. For a list of those known to have attended the jubilee, see Martha W. England, *Garrick and Stratford*, New York, 1962. Appendix B, 67–69.

[2] *Boswell in Search of a Wife*, 282.

[3] *The Gentleman's Magazine*, Sept. 1769, 39, 422.

add to the entertainment of the guests at the ball superb fireworks[1] were let off on the bank of the river under the supervision of Mr Angelo. Strangely enough, the handbills distributed in the morning as well as the final programme for the three days do not include any fireworks on Wednesday night, and only a few London papers mention them. The great display of fireworks was planned as a climax before the masquerade the next evening, but obviously Angelo must have been eager to give the public a preview of what to expect the next night.

Everybody was delighted with the first day, and all agreed that the whole affair was conducted with the greatest decorum and gave great satisfaction. The fireworks, the illuminated houses, the large transparencies, the beautifully dressed dancers, all contributed to a very pleasing and exciting spectacle. In fact, the first day of the Jubilee was a very great success. The participants could retire to their lodgings for a few hours' rest, as one of them wrote, 'I came away with the rest, and devoted in a bed miserable in every particular, but that it was clean, a few hours to peaceful oblivion.'[2]

2. THE SECOND DAY

The beginning of the festivities on Thursday, September the 7th was, as on the previous day, announced by the firing of cannon followed by the serenading of the ladies. All the most important entertainments were planned for this day, and early in the morning handbills had been distributed with the programme. They read:

[1] Wheler, op. cit., 173.
[2] *The Gentleman's Magazine*, Sept. 1769, **39**, 422.

SECOND DAY

The STEWARD of the JUBILEE informs the
Company that at nine o'clock will be a
PUBLIC BREAKFAST
at the TOWN HALL
At Eleven o'Clock, a PAGEANT
(if the Weather will permit) to proceed
from the *College* to the *Amphitheatre*
Where An ODE
(upon dedicating a BUILDING and erecting
a STATUE to the Memory of SHAKE-
SPEARE) will be performed after which
the PAGEANT will return to the *College*.
At FOUR an ORDINARY for *Ladies* and *Gentlemen*.
At EIGHT, the FIREWORKS.
And at ELEVEN o'Clock
The MASQUERADE.[1]

But unfortunately the weather had become unsettled
during the night; 'a hateful drizzling rain' kept coming
down, completely ruining the possibility of any outdoor
activities before noon. Some people thought that the
change in the weather was caused by the passing of the
famous Halley's comet, which with its brightly shining
tail had been plainly visible the night before and had
struck the spectators at Stratford with awe; for according
to public superstition the appearance of a comet was
interpreted as an omen for some coming disaster.

This morning no breakfast was served at the amphitheatre, which was being made ready for the performance
of the Dedication Ode. At the Town Hall the breakfast
crowd was alarmed by the rain. Garrick was obliged to
have new handbills printed and distributed in a hurry

[1] Victor, op. cit., 3, 214-15.

to announce the following changes in the arrangements:

To the
Ladies and Gentlemen
at the
Jubilee
Thursday Sep. 7th 1769
As the weather proves so unfavourable for the
PAGEANT
The Steward begs leave to inform them that it is
obliged to be deferr'd.
THE ODE
will be perform'd at 12 in the Amphitheatre,
The Doors to be open'd at 11.[1]

Garrick's disappointment was great, but he managed to
keep up a brave front when he was with company, although so many things went wrong. Cradock mentions
one added annoyance:

The man who was to shave him, perhaps not quite sober, absolutely cut him from the corner of his mouth to his chin . . . the
ladies were engaged in applying constant stiptics to stop the
bleeding.[2]

To have this accident happen on the very day that he had
to appear in all his glory reciting the Dedication Ode
was most disconcerting, and Mrs Garrick had to use all
her tact and skill with her annoyed husband. He was
much concerned about the fate of the planned procession
of 170 people costumed as characters from Shakespeare's
plays, with most of their apparel borrowed from the Drury
Lane wardrobe. It had been the most difficult and the

---

[1] David Garrick, *The Jubilee* (pp. 55–113) in Elizabeth P. Stein, *Three
Plays by David Garrick*, New York, 1926, 62.

[2] Cradock, op. cit., I, 217.

F

most expensive to arrange of all the entertainments
planned. Wild confusion reigned at the College, where
the procession was being marshalled for eleven o'clock.
It was postponed till two o'clock in the hope that the
rain would have stopped by then. But the showers continued, and it was finally decided to postpone the pageant
till the next day. Henry Angelo gives the following
account of all this:

The elements, however, . . . went on with their work, regardless
of the comfort or convenience of these mock-kings and pseudo-
heroes. It appeared the rather, as if the clouds, in an ill humour
with these magnificent doings, had sucked up a super-abundance
of water, to shower down upon the finery of the mimic host, and
that the river gods had opened all the sluices of the Avon, to drown
the devotees of her boasted bard. . . . Lacy [the co-manager of the
Drury Lane], as the story goes, was cruelly angry at the watery
gods, exclaiming to Garrick, 'See – who the devil, Davy, would
venture upon the procession under such lowering aspects? Sir, all
the ostrich feathers will be spoiled, and the *property* will be damni-
fied five thousand pounds.'[1]

Boswell remarks that: 'The heavy Rains made it impossible to have this [i.e. the procession] exhibited without
destroying the valuable Dresses, and endangering the
still more valuable Health of the fair Performers.'[2]
Cradock, critical as usual, held a slightly different
opinion and wrote many years later:

And it was not altogether unfortunate that the weather was
stormy and tempestuous, as it formed an excuse for no procession
to be expected to pass through the streets, for if any dresses had
arrived, they were of such a sort as would by no means have borne
either day-light or any near examination; and here, the ever-

[1] Angelo, op. cit., I, 48.
[2] *The Public Advertiser*, Sept. 16, 1769, 2, col. 3.

ready Mr. Foote might be a little disappointed, perhaps, for he had
aptly enough prepared the following alliterative couplet:

To solemn sounds see sordid Scene-Men stalk
And the great Shakespeare's vast Creation — walk![1]

According to the original plan the procession, led by the
band, would start from the College and then march
through the streets to the birthplace, 'and sing an Air,
which began with these Lines,

> From Clouds he broke forth,
> To enlighten the Earth
> And spread all his Glory around . . .'[2]

This is not found in *Shakespeare's Garland*, which has
the following chorus marked for the pageant:

> HENCE ye prophane! and only they,
> Our pageant grace our pomp survey,
> Whom love of sacred genius brings;
> Let pride, let flattery decree,
> Honors to deck the memory,
> Of warriors, senators, and kings —
> Not less in glory, and desert,
> The poet here receives his part,
> A tribute from the feeling heart.[3]

From the birthplace the procession was to go to the
Amphitheatre. There the participants were to place
themselves in front of the the orchestra, where the statue
of Shakespeare, Garrick's gift to Stratford, had been
erected a little towards the back, but in the centre line,
towering over the rows. This would have made an impressive spectacle for the presentation of the Dedication

[1] Cradock, op. cit., 1, 217.
[2] Victor, op. cit., 3, 208.
[3] *Shakespeare's Garland*, 17.

Ode, which now would have to be performed without such a picturesque support. The doors were opened an hour before the performance, which was to begin at noon, and soon the hall, which would conveniently hold one thousand, was overcrowded; some even estimated the audience at about twice that number.

Mᵣ Garrick reciting the Ode, in honor of Shakspeare, at the Jubilee at Stratford; with the Musical Performers &c.

Garrick reciting the Ode at Stratford
(from *The Town and Country Magazine*, Sept. 1769)

A remarkable thing happened. In spite of the unexpected misfortunes with which Garrick had had to contend, and they were legion, by superb self-control and drawing on all his inner strength and his skill as an actor, he managed on this occasion to appear poised, untroubled and even gay, thereby turning what might have been a near failure into an overwhelming success for himself by his superb performance of the Dedication Ode.

The whole Drury Lane band and all the singers also

had their part in this. The Ode had been set to music by
Dr Arne, who himself conducted the orchestra. Wearing
a dress similar to Garrick's 'he stood on the left side of
the statue in order the more conveniently to regulate the
band'.[1] (See facing page and Plate 8.)

. . . in the Front of this Orchestra, with the Steward's Rod in his
Hand and with his Medallion about his Neck, Mr. Garrick sat
dressed in a suit of brown, with a rich Gold Lace; he opened the
Performance with a very respectful Bow to the Company which
was returned with a very respectful Clap of unanimous Applause,
and at the End of each Recitative Part he sat down, and gave the
Singer an Opportunity of displaying his or her Abilities.[2]

Then the music began, and to the great surprise of the
audience Garrick *spoke* the first recitative:[3]

> To what blest genius of the isle
> Shall Gratitude her tribute pay,
> Decree the festive day,
> Erect the statue, and devote the pile?[4] (p. 1.)

A rather tame opening but soon he gathered force:

> 'Tis he! 'tis he! – that demi-god!
> Who Avon's flow'ry margin trod,
> While sportive *Fancy* round him flew,
> Where *Nature* led him by the hand,
> Instructed him in all she knew,
> And gave him absolute command!

[1] Wheler, op. cit., 174.

[2] *The St James Chronicle*, Sept. 9–12, 1769, 4, col. 2.

[3] Victor, op. cit., 3, 216, notes that 'Garrick was the first who conceived the
Idea of Speaking the Recitative, which in general is the most languid and
neglected Part of a musical Performance'.

[4] For the full text of the Ode, see D[avid] G[arrick], *An | Ode | upon | dedi-
cating a Building, | and | erecting a Statue | to | Shakespeare, | at | Stratford-
upon-Avon. | London | Printed for T. Becket, and P. A. De Hondt, in the
Strand. | 1769; also in Wheler, op. cit., 175–85.*

'Tis he! 'Tis he!
'The god of our idolatry!'
To him the song, the Edifice we raise;
He merits all our wonder, all our praise! (pp. 1–2.)

In the next stanza he urged the audience to restrain their joy for a short time:

Let awful silence still the air!
From the dark cloud the hidden light
    Bursts tenfold bright!
Prepare! Prepare! Prepare!
Now swell the choral song,
Roll the full tide of harmony along;
    Let rapture sweep the trembling strings,
    And Fame expanding all her wings,
With all her trumpet-tongues proclaim
The lov'd, rever'd, immortal name!
SHAKESPEARE! SHAKESPEARE! SHAKESPEARE! (p. 2.)

Then Garrick sat down and here the full chorus came in with an abbreviated version of the last part of the recitative:

The lov'd, rever'd, immortal name!
SHAKESPEARE! SHAKESPEARE! SHAKESPEARE!

At this point the first air was introduced, a light pastoral with echoes from Milton:

Sweetest bard that ever *sung,*
Nature's *glory,* Fancy's *child;*
Never sure did witching tongue,
    Warble forth such wood-notes wild!

Come each Muse *and sister* Grace
    Loves *and* Pleasures *hither come;*
Well you know this happy place,
    Avon's *banks were once your home.*

Bring the laurel, bring the flow'rs
Songs of triumph to him raise;
He united all your pow'rs,
All uniting, sing his praise! (pp. 3–4.)

Thereupon Garrick arose for the second recitative, in which he contrasted with Shakespeare 'Philip's fam'd unconquer'd son' Alexander, who was despondent, because there were no more new worlds for him to conquer:

But when our SHAKESPEARE's matchless pen,
Like ALEXANDER's sword, had done with men,
He heav'd no sigh, he made no moan;
    Not limited to human kind,
    He fir'd his wonder-teeming mind,
Rais'd other worlds, and beings of his own! (p. 4.)

The second brief air followed, after which Garrick went on to tell:

. . . how sitting on his magic throne,
    Unaided and alone,
        In dreadful state,
    The subject passions round him wait;
    What though unchain'd, and raging there,
He checks, inflames, or turns their mad career;
        With that superior skill,
    Which winds the fiery steed at will,
    He gives the awful word —
And they, all foaming, trembling, own him for their lord.

— With these his slaves he can controul,
        Or charm the soul;
    So realiz'd are all his golden dreams
        Of terror, pity, love, and grief,
    Though conscious that the vision only seems,
    The woe-struck mind finds no relief:

Ingratitude would drop the tear,
Cold-blooded age take fire,
To see the thankless children of old *Lear*
Spurn at their king and sire!
With *his* our reason too grows wild!
What Nature had disjoin'd,
The Poet's pow'r combin'd
Madness and age, ingratitude and child! (pp. 5–6.)

The next recitative forms a transition from the horrors of tragedy to the mirth of comedy:

The scene is chang'd, — Thalia comes,
Leading the nymph Euphrosyne,
Goddess of joy and liberty!

She and her sisters circle 'the monarch of th'inchanted land'. Then the fourth air, one of mirth, is sung:

Wild, frantic with pleasure,
They trip it in measure,
To bring him their treasure,
The treasure of joy! (p. 8.)

The recitative following made a very deep impression and was by many considered the best part of the Ode:

... *Fancy*, *Wit* and *Humour* spread
Their wings, and hover round his head,
Impregnating his mind.
Which teeming soon, as soon brought forth,
Not a tiny spurious birth,
But out a mountain came,
A mountain of delight!
LAUGHTER roar'd out to see the sight,
And FALSTAFF was his name!
With sword and shield he, puffing, strides;
The joyous revel-rout
Receive him with a shout,
And modest *Nature* holds her sides:

> No single pow'r the deed has done,
>> But great and small,
> *Wit, Fancy, Humour, Whim,* and *Jest,*
> The huge, mishapen [*sic*] heap impress'd;
>> And lo! — SIR JOHN!
>> A compound of 'em all,
>>> A comic world in ONE. (pp. 9–10.)

The fifth air picks up the theme:

> *A world where all pleasures abound,*
>> *So fruitful the earth,*
>> *So quick to bring forth,*
> *And the world too is wicked and round . . .*

> *So* FALSTAFF *will never decline:*
>> *Still fruitful and gay,*
>> *He moistens his clay,*
> *And his rain and his rivers are wine.*

> *Of the world he had all, but its care;*
> *No load, but of flesh, will he bear;*
>> *He laughs off his pack,*
>> *Takes a cup of old sack,*
> *And away with all sorrow and care.* (p. 10.)

The next recitative praises the River Avon, setting it above the Thames, the Isis, and the Cam. When it was finished Mrs Baddeley, who had an exquisite voice, sang the sixth air, which had such instant success that it had to be repeated. Just before the encore Garrick had the doors of the Amphitheatre facing the river flung wide open to the torrent of rain outside.[1] By now he felt that he had complete control of his audience and could allow himself that theatrical gesture, laughing at the stormy weather and savouring the ironical situation, as once more the singer began:

[1] Dibdin, op. cit., I, 76.

Thou soft-flowing Avon, *by thy silver stream,*
Of things more than mortal, sweet Shakespeare would dream,
The fairies by moonlight dance round his green bed,
For hallow'd the turf is which pillow'd his head.

. . . . . .

Flow on, silver Avon! *in song ever flow,*
Be the swans on thy bosom still whiter than snow,
Ever full be thy stream. . . . (pp. 12–13.)

The Avon certainly complied with the wish on that day. The stream was full, beginning to overflow its banks in the meadow at the Amphitheatre and spreading rapidly. But nobody paid any attention to that, for Mrs Baddeley's singing completely charmed the entranced audience. In the next recitative Garrick mentioned the tribute that other poets had paid to Shakespeare. A brief gentle air followed, whereupon he turned towards the statue with these words:

Look down, blest SPIRIT! from above,
With all thy wonted gentleness and love;
     And as the wonders of thy pen,
          By heav'n inspir'd,
          To virtue fir'd,
     The charm'd, astonish'd, sons of men!
With no reproach, even now, thou view'st thy work,
     To nature sacred as to truth,
     Where no alluring mischiefs lurk,
          To taint the mind of youth.
Still to thy native spot thy smiles extend
And as thou gav'st it fame, that fame defend. (pp. 14–15.)

. . . . . .

Can *British* gratitude delay
     To him, the glory of this isle,
     To give the festive day,
The song, the statue, and devoted pile?
To *him*, the first of poets, best of men?
'*We ne'er shall look upon his like again!*' (p. 15.)

This theme was picked up in a four-line duet followed by the final chorus:

> We will his brows with laurel bind,
> Who charms to virtue human kind:
> Raise the pile, the statue raise,
> Sing immortal Shakespeare's praise!
> The song will cease, the stone decay,
> But HIS name,
> And undiminish'd fame
> Shall never, never pass away!

Numerous reports from members of the audience all show that Garrick's delivery of the Ode, often interrupted by 'turbulent applause', was received with the greatest enthusiasm and admiration. Only a few of them will be quoted. 'A Friend to true Merit' writes from Stratford on September the 12th, stressing the emotional impact of the Ode:

The Deportment of Mr. Garrick struck an Awe on everyone present . . . the Stillness and Attention was never so remarkable, and when he opened the Ode, his enchanting Powers caught hold of your very Soul. The Passions, perhaps, were never so truly painted! . . . The Powers he shewed in the tenderest Feelings of human Nature, drew from the Audience in general the best Testimony of their Feelings, for I will take it upon me to say, scarce a dry Eye was seen – and before the Audience could well dry up their sympathetic Tears, his comic Powers rushed upon the Character of Falstaff, that incessant Bursts of Laughter filled the Amphitheatre. You will, Mr. Printer, excuse the Overflowings of a grateful Heart on this Occasion; it falls very short of what is due to the Excellence of so great a Master of the Human Passions.[1]

In the same issue of *The Public Advertiser* Boswell writes with his usual ebullience:

[1] *The Public Advertiser*, Sept. 16, 1769, 3, col. 1.

The Performance of the Dedication Ode was noble and affecting
. . . and I do believe, that if any one [such as Samuel Foote] had
attempted to disturb the Performance, he would have been in
Danger of his Life . . . Garrick, . . . inspired with an awful
Elevation of Soul, while he looked, from Time to Time, at the
venerable Statute of Shakespeare, appeared more than himself.
While he repeated the Ode, and saw the various Passions and Feelings, which it contains, fully transfused into all around him, he
seemed in Extacy, and gave us the Idea of a Mortal transformed
into a Demi-god, as we read in the Pagan Mythology.

I can witness from my own Hearing, what did great Honour to
Lord Grosvenor, as well as to Mr. Garrick. After the Ode his
Lordship came up to the Orchestra, and told Mr. Garrick, that
he had affected his whole Frame, showing him his Veins and
Nerves still quivering with Agitation. What truly delighted me was
to observe the warm Sincerity of Mr. Garrick's Enthusiasm for
his immortal Bard, throughout the whole Suite of Entertainments;
. . . and the Triumph of his Countenance at some Parts of the
Ode, its Tenderness at others, and inimitable sly Humour at
others, cannot be described.[1]

Another enthusiastic eye-witness account is quoted by
Wheler:

I must express my great satisfaction, at the agreeable manner Mr.
Garrick *spoke* the Ode, thereby exalting his performance above
criticism. When I saw the statue of Shakespeare, the greatest
dramatic poet, and the living person of Garrick, the greatest actor
that England ever produced; when I considered the occasion, the
scene, and the company that was drawn together by the power of
one man, I was struck with a kind of veneration and enthusiasm,
and the same sentiments, I make no doubt, operating in the
breasts of others, contributed greatly to the applause the performance met with.[2]

[1] *The Public Advertiser*, Sept. 16, 1769, 2, col. 1.
[2] Wheler, op. cit., 174.

Wheler reprints the Ode in full, mentions the delight given by the air 'Thou soft-flowing Avon' and that the part dealing with the passions 'deserved the applause which was bestowed upon it' and continues:

. . . and to some this was the most enchanting part of the whole: he was Falstaff himself. . . . The company was in raptures, when the speaker began '*Look down blest spirit from above*' and the concluding chorus wanted only the action of crowning the statue to have rendered the whole complete. In short, it was allowed by all who had the happiness to be present at the recital of this Ode, that there never was exhibited in England, a performance more pleasing, more grand, or more worthy the memory of Shakespeare; and in which the genius and talents of Garrick (by whose enchanting powers it was rendered superior to criticism) was so thoroughly admirable, and gave so perfect a satisfaction. In the performance of this Ode, Mr. Garrick distinguished himself equally as a poet, an actor, and a gentleman.[1]

Some visitors mentioned that Garrick had greatly surpassed the expectations of his friends in his composition and performance of the Ode; one of them gives it high praise:

. . . his introduction of Falstaff, accompanied by all his power of voice, face and gesture, compelled such applause as I never heard before; his saying that the fat knight is 'a comic world in one!' 'And the world too is wicked and round!' surely is genuine wit. I could dwell for ever on the Ode, which received every advantage that the greatest orator of the age, himself the author, could give. Nor should Dr. Arne's incomparable taste in the musical parts be forgot. . . .[2]

Boswell makes the following comment:

[1] Wheler, op. cit., 186–7.
[2] *The Gentleman's Magazine*, Sept. 1769, 39, 422.

I know not whether it may be a Compliment to Mr. Garrick, but I must say, that his Ode greatly exceeded my Expectations. I knew his Talents for little sportive Sallies, but I feared that a Dedication Ode for Shakespeare was above his Powers. What the Critics may say of the Performance, I know not, but I shall never be induced to waver in my Opinion of it. I am sensible of its Defects; but upon the whole I think it a Work of superior Merit, well suited to the Occasion by the Variety of its Subjects and containing both Force and Elegance. It would be unpardonable should I omit acknowledging the Pleasure which I received from Dr. Arne's Music, which was truly fine; nor must I neglect thanking the whole Orchestra for their Execution.[1]

What the critics did say later about the Ode was certainly not very complimentary, but we can judge the powerful effect on the audience by the fact that even Dibdin allows himself to be enthusiastic about the performance of the Ode, although he cannot refrain from adding a poisoned barb. After quoting extensively from Boswell's account, he continues:

. . . if he had added that there was never enthusiasm so ardently conveyed, nor so worthily felt; that it was magic; that it was fairy land; and that when the doors of the Amphitheatre were thrown open, and the river AVON was discovered at the very moment when the symphony 'Thou sweet-flowing Avon' begun, the effect was irresistible, electrical; that every soul present felt it, cherished it, delighted in it, and considered that moment as the most endearing to sensibility that could possibly be experienced, when he had said this and ten times more, he would only have given a very faint idea of the real impression.

But all this does not take off the force, or contradict the truth, of my assertion. If GARRICK felt all this extasy and imparted it to his auditors . . . I know that it was called forth by a contemplation of the prodigious remuneration that would result to himself.

[1] *The Public Advertiser*, Sept. 16, 1769, 2, col. 1.

. . . It was acting; and while he was infusing into the very souls
of his hearers the merits of the incomparable Shakespear . . . his
soul was fixed upon the DRURY-LANE treasury. I will give him all
that has been said, and twenty times more, as to the enchantment
and the fascination of his admirable powers of acting, but let no
man tell me that at the very moment he uttered the line 'We shall
not look upon his like again,' the manner and effect of which
beggared all description, he did not feel that the jubilee would be
performed half of the following season at DRURY-LANE theatre.[1]

Cradock briefly mentions that 'under all discouragement,
the Ode went off much better than could have been expected, and Garrick found himself surrounded by a most
judicious circle of friends, as well as splendid fashionable
admirers'.[2]

When the applause had subsided Garrick made a
polite address to the audience, in which he lamented that
none of the poets of the Universities, more capable than
himself, had been willing to undertake that arduous task
of writing the Ode, and 'expressed an apprehension, that
his zeal for the honour of Shakespeare had led him to
expose the weakness of his own abilities, but hoped his
motive would apologize for defects'.[3] He stressed the
fact:

that he found it quite another Thing to speak in Public, supported
by the great Genius of Shakespeare, from what he found it to
speak in Public, supported only by his own feeble Genius; but
he hoped we would shew him the same kind Indulgence, as is
usually shown to those unfortunate Gentlemen, who appear for
the first time in a character.[4]

---

[1] Dibdin, op. cit., I, 76–77.
[2] Cradock, op. cit., I, 217–18.
[3] *The Town and Country Magazine*, Sept. 1769, I, 474–5.
[4] *The Public Advertiser*, Sept. 16, 1769, 2, col. 2.

Turning to Dr Arne, he politely added that he himself, however,

had one consolation; that the first musical genius of this country did not think his muse unworthy of the exercise of his talents, and that he was certain the composer's excellence would amply attone [*sic*] for the imperfections of the author.[1]

Then, looking at the statue, he recited Milton's poem:

> What needs my Shakespeare for his honoured bones,
> The labour of an age in piled stones? . . .
> Dear son of memory, great heir of fame,
> What need'st thou such weak witness of thy name?
> Thou in our wonder and astonishment
> Hast built thyself a livelong monument.

From this point on there is a slight uncertainty about the order of events and the exact time when Garrick delivered his Oration on Shakespeare. Most newspaper and magazine writers make the following brief statement:

When the Ode was finished, Mr. Garrick stood up, and delivered a Prose Encomium on Shakespeare, in which the Poet's enemies were called upon to urge whatever they could advance in Opposition to his Character.[2]

This must refer to *An Oration in Honour of Shakespeare*, which had been printed in full in several newspapers on September the 4th and the 5th, as 'intended to be spoken by Mr. Garrick'. Wheler, who in 1806 included the text of the oration in his book on Stratford, mentions it as 'written and spoken by Mr. Garrick', but this seems to be an error. It should be noted that Garrick never claimed

---

[1] *The Town and Country Magazine*, Sept. 1769, 1, 475.
[2] *The St James Chronicle*, Sept. 9–12, 1769, 4, col. 2.

that he had written the Oration himself; that it was never ascribed to him by his contemporaries; and that it was never published for sale separately, but appeared only in the newspapers and magazines. Garrick did not have the technical skill or the ability to write a formal oration, although he could be trusted to deliver one well; thus he must have sought professional assistance. There is, however, no external evidence to show whom Garrick consulted. An interesting hypothesis, based on internal evidence only, that the collaborator was his friend Edmund Burke, has recently been advanced by Mrs Martha W. England in her book *Garrick and Stratford*.[1] A detailed analysis of the oration, and a comparison of its style with the characteristics of style found in other prose writings by Garrick and Burke, leads her to maintain that the opening paragraphs and the closing ones are in the theatrical manner characteristic of Garrick, whereas the whole central part shows the grand oratorical style characteristic of Burke.[2] The Oration, with its echoes of Pope and of Johnson's 'Preface to Shakespeare', does contain some sound Shakespeare criticism; and as it is not easily available, the text is reproduced here, except for the last two paragraphs, which seem to a modern reader singularly vague and trite, not to say inane.

AN ORATION
IN HONOUR OF SHAKESPEARE

'*The only science of mankind is man.*' This is the aphorism of an author, who has been equally admired as a philosopher and a poet; and if it is allowed, that man is the fittest object of our study; the drama, which exhibits the passions and pursuits of man, stands in

[1] Martha W. England, *Garrick and Stratford*, New York, 1962.
[2] Ibid., 41–43.

G

the first class of literary composition. Shakespeare is, above all others, allowed to be the poet of nature; and therefore, as an author, he stands highest in the highest class. The beings exhibited by the poet of nature, are *men*: they are not creatures of the imagination, acting from principles by which human actions were never produced, and suffering distress which human beings never suffered; but partakers of the same nature with ourselves, to whose hearts our own sensations are a clue; being of like passions, impelled by the same hopes and fears, and sacrificing virtue to interest, or interest to virtue, as circumstances concur with disposition, and opinion connects present and immediate good and evil with future, either by necessary consequence, or judicial determination.

But the contemplation of man, as exhibited by the poet upon the stage, is of more advantage than as passing before us in the scenes of life. In the world we see only the actions of mankind, and before we can infer any useful knowledge from them, we must investigate their motives, and often suspend our judgment of the consequences till they appear in a distant event. But in the scenes where men are exhibited by the poet, we see at once their action, and its secret springs, which being thus connected, as effects and cause, we are afterwards able to refer conduct into passions and principles; we see also upon the stage the final events in which the whole concatenation of motive and action terminates; which enable us to look through life with a kind of prescient sagacity, and discover the effects of human action in their cause.

But Shakespeare does not only teach us what it is most our interest to know; for by the very manner in which he conveys the most important knowledge, he gives us the most rational refined, and exquisite delight. He has not delineated a chart, but painted a picture: – he shews us the path of life, not by geometrical line, but by perspective, and elevation: – he does not personify human passions, and exhibit them, either separate or combined, as they would appear abstracted from the modes of life; he '*catches the manners living as they rise*:' he paints character, not merely as resulting from different turns of disposition, and degrees of understanding, but from situation and habit. Their passions and principles are indeed general, but they act and speak with the peculiarities of a class, though not of an individual. Shallow and Falstaff differ as much in the consequence of circumstances, that made one a justice and one a soldier, as of any radical and native turn of mind; and the originals in nature, from which these portraits were drawn, are as well known now as they were then; the difference which custom has produced in the language and modes of life, is but like the different dresses, in which the same air and features will always be distinguished. Justice Shallow is still to be found, though he has changed his coat; he still boasts of midnight frolics, though it is not now the custom of rakes to sleep in the windmill in St. George's Fields; and of familiarity with the great, though there is no object of puny ambition called John of Gaunt.

We get knowledge from Shakespeare, not with painful labour as we dig gold from the mine, but at leisure, and with delight, as we gain health and vigour from the sports of the field. A picture frequently pleases which represents an object, that in itself is disgustful. Teniers represents a number of Dutch boors, drunk and quarrelling in a wretched hovel, and we admire the piece for a kind of relative beauty, as a just imitation of life and nature: with this beauty we are struck in Shakespeare; we know his originals, and contemplate the truth of his copy with delight.

It was happy for Shakespeare, and for us, that in his time there was no example by the imitation of which he might hope to be approved. He painted nature as it appeared to his own eye, and not from a transcript of what was seen in nature by another. The genius looks not *upon* nature, but *through* it; not at the outline only, but the differences, nice and innumerable within it: at all that the variation of tints, and the endless combinations of light and shade can express. As the power of perception is more, more is still perceived in the inexhaustible varieties of life; but to copy only what another has seen, is to render superior perspicacity vain, and neither the painter, nor the poet, can hope to excell, who is content to reflect a reflection, and to seek for nothing in nature, which others have not found.

But there are beauties in Shakespeare not relative; powers that do not imitate, but create. *He was as another nature*: he represents not only actions that were not performed, but beings that do not exist; yet to these beings he assigns not only faculties, but character; he gives them not only peculiar dispositions, but characteristic modes of expressing them: they have character, not merely from the passions and understanding, but from situation and habit; Caliban and Ariel, like Shallow and Falstaff, are not more strongly distinguished, in consequence of different natures, than of different circumstances and employments.

As there was no poet to seduce Shakespeare into imitation, there was no critic to restrain his extravagance; yet we find the force of his own judgment sufficient to rein his imagination, and reduce to system the new world which he made.

Does anyone now enquire whether Shakespeare was learned? do they mean whether he knew how to call the same thing by several names? for learning, with respect to language, teaches no more. Learning, in its best sense, is only nature at the rebound; it is only the discovery of what is; and he who looks upon nature with a penetrating eye, derives learning from the source. Rules of poetry have been deduced from examples, and not examples from rules; as a poet, therefore, Shakespeare did not need books; and in no instance in which he needed them as a philosopher, or historian, does he appear ignorant of what they teach.

His language, like his conceptions, is strongly marked with the characteristic of nature; it is bold, figurative, and significant; his terms rather than his sentences are metaphorical; he calls an endless multitude a sea, by a happy allusion to the perpetual succession of wave to wave; and he immediately expresses opposition, by taking up arms; which, being fit in itself, he was not solicitous to accommodate to his first image: this is the language in which a figurative and rapid conception will always be expressed: this is the language both of the prophet, and the poet, of native eloquence, and divine inspiration.

It has been objected to Shakespeare that he wrote without any moral purpose, but I boldly reply, that he has effected a thousand: he has not, indeed, always contrived a series of events, from the whole of which some moral precept may be inferred, but he has conveyed some rule of conduct, some principle of knowledge, not only in almost every speech of his dialogue, but in every incident, character, and event. Thus great was Shakespeare, as he appears in his *works*; but in *himself* he was greater still. The genius in every art, has an idea of perfection which he cannot attain: this idea, beyond what others can conceive, and a perpetual effort to reach it, produce that excellence which distinguishes his works; but Shakespeare appears to have despised his performances when he compared them, not only with his ideas, but his powers; for how else can we account for his taking no care to collect them: when he saw part of them corruptly published by others, he neither amended the faults, nor secured the rest from the same injury. It appears, therefore, 'that he judged those works unworthy to be preserved, by restoring and explaining which, the critics of succeeding ages were to contend for fame'.

Thus, without the incentive of future reputation, without any other exertion of his powers than would satisfy an audience wholly unacquainted with the drama, he has excited universal admiration, as the sun becomes glorious by the spontaneous effusions of his rays.

Is there any here whose attention has been fixed, whose imagination filled, and whose passions moved by other scenes, as they have been fixed, filled and moved by the scenes of Shakespeare? 'if there be any, speak! for him have I offended'. . . .[1]

It is surprising that there is practically no comment on the Oration and its effect on the audience by anybody present. Is it possible that people were too emotionally exhausted after the performance of the Ode to give it full attention, or that Garrick suddenly decided not to deliver the full Oration at all? We shall never know.

Victor gives a vivid account of the next events, when Garrick once more addressed the company:

[1] Wheler, op. cit., 191–5.

Your *Attendance* here upon this Occasion is a Proof that you have felt . . . his Genius! and that you love and revere him and his Memory – the only remaining Honour to him now (and it is the greatest Honour you can do him) is to SPEAK for him [Here a Pause ensued with a general Laugh] – Perhaps my Proposition (continued he) comes a little too abruptly upon you? With your Permission, we will desire the Gentlemen [the Band of Music] to give you time, by a Piece of Music, to recollect and adjust your thoughts. [After the Piece of Music] Now Ladies and Gentlemen, will you be pleased to say any Thing *for* or *against* SHAKESPEARE.[1]

A man muffled in a greatcoat, standing in direct line with the orchestra, declared his intention of attacking Shakespeare. The audience gasped with surprise. 'He went around and (speedily taking off his coat) came out in the orchestra, in a suit of fashionable blue with silver frogs, to support the justice of his allegations.'[2] Many recognized Thomas King, next to Garrick the best-loved actor at Drury Lane, and the blue suit in which he had appeared as a Macaroni, or Frenchified fop, in several plays – for instance as Lord Ogleby in Garrick and Colman's play *The Clandestine Marriage*. (See illustration, facing p. 88.) In a high-pitched voice with mincing, affected speech, 'he tried the force of his ingenuity to decry and ridicule Shakespeare and his writings, together with the Jubilee in his honour'. He stated as his chief objection to Shakespeare:

. . . his being a vulgar author, who excites those common emotions of laughing and crying, which were entirely indecent and unbecoming in polite assemblies; that the criterion of a fine gentleman was to be moved at nothing – to feel nothing – to admire nothing. . . . He owned that he did not much love his

[1] Victor, op. cit., 3, 218–19.
[2] *The Town and Country Magazine*, Sept. 1769, I, 475.

Thomas King and Mrs Baddeley, in *The Clandestine Marriage*

(Oil painting in the possession of the Garrick Club)

Dr Arne
(Engraving from a drawing by Bartolozzi)

country — yet he could wish that it would submit to become civilised and as the first step never to suffer so execrable a fellow as Shakespeare with his things called comedies and tragedies to debauch their minds and understandings, and produce *snivelings* and *horse-laughs* when the chief excellence of man, and the most refined Sensation, was to be devoured by *ennui*, and only live in a state of vegetation. . . .[1]

In his arguments he combined Voltaire's accusations against Shakespeare, particularly against his 'barbarity' with the derogatory criticisms of Shakespeare, but chiefly of the planned Jubilee and its steward, that Garrick's enemies (foremost among them the commentator George Steevens) had published in *The Public Advertiser* and other papers in the months before the Jubilee.

The audience was confused by all this:

Those who knew him [Mr King] expected something extremely whimsical, while many who did not, testified the greatest Amazement at so unexpected an Attack upon the first dramatic Poet of their Country. . . . Several, who thought he was really serious, seemed exceedingly dissatisfied with him, while Numbers, who saw into the Intention, were highly diverted, and testified a satisfaction proportioned to the Astonishment expressed by the less informed Part of the Auditory.[2]

Of course this whole episode was not spontaneous, but had been carefully staged by Garrick. Cradock mentions that he even had some of the performers in the orchestra interrupt and attempt to reply to Mr King's malicious remarks about the Steward and the Jubilee, and 'that this produced no effect, certainly no good one'.[3]

[1] Davies, op. cit., vol. 4, pp. 228–9. (De Luxe ed.) Also Victor, op. cit., vol. 3, pp. 221–2. I have combined these two quotations.
[2] *The St James Chronicle*, Sept. 9–12, 1769, 4, col. 2.
[3] Cradock, op. cit., 1, 218.

Garrick had been irked by all the newspaper attacks, many of them scurrilous or absurd, on the coming Jubilee and its Steward. His Oration and Mr King's performance was his answer to the critics. By introducing the Frenchified fop, or Macaroni, as an opponent of Shakespeare, at a moment when enthusiasm for the poet was approaching idolatry, he made him and all other opponents appear ridiculous. Boswell sensed Garrick's intention and deplored it:

Mr. King . . . gave a smart ironical attack upon Shakespeare in the Character of a modern refined Man of Taste. This might have done well on some other Occasion; but in my Opinion, it had better have been omitted at this noble Festival: It detracted from it's Dignity; nor was there any Occasion for it. We were enthusiastic Admirers of Shakespeare. We had not Time to think of his cavilling Critics. We were wrapped into Wonder and Admiration of our immortal Bard; and the Levity of the fine Gentleman disturbed the Tone of our Minds. I must be forgiven too for observing, that this Exhibition looked so like a Trap laid on Purpose, that it displeased me; and I was angry to find any Notice taken of the venomous Insects, who have shot their stings in the News-Papers against the Jubilee, and particularly against Mr. Garrick. It had the Appearance of a Soreness unworthy of our Lord-High-Steward . . . I must however do Justice to Tom King, and allow that he played his Part exceedingly well.[1]

Another visitor, however, was very critical of Mr King's performance:

I did not admire it, probably for want of taste. Mr. King is undoubtedly an excellent Comedian upon the Stage, but as an *Orator* in a public Assembly he appears deficient, and to speak well extempore, upon an Occasion rather new and uncommon, requires very different Talents. There was something *smart* now

[1] *The Public Advertiser*, Sept. 16, 1769, 2, col. 2.

and then in his speech, but upon the whole, it sunk into the *insipid*, and I could wish that part of the Entertainment had been let alone.[1]

In contrast to this view, others comment on Mr King's 'genuine humour and admirable acting' which 'produced much mirth and was a considerable addition to the entertainment'.[2]

An unfortunate accident occurred during the performance. On account of the serious overcrowding, 'benches in various parts of the theatre gave way; . . . and had it not been for a peculiar interposition of Providence, Lord Carlisle, who was much hurt by the fall of a door, must have inevitably been destroyed'.[3]

When King had finished, Garrick addressed him and the audience with polite sarcasm:

I must beg leave in the name of all Admirers of Shakespeare to return our Thanks to that very fine and refin'd Gentleman and Critic for the great Panegyrick he has pleas'd to bestow upon their Favourite . . . I hope we are *not yet refin'd* enough to accept of this Gentleman's Proposals for the improving our Theatre, but that we shall Entertain and content ourselves with that Heav'n has sent us in SHAKESPEARE.

O Ladies! It is You and You alone can put a Stop to this terrible progress and irruption of the Anti-Goths. *It was You Ladies* that restor'd Shakespeare to the Stage, you form'd yourselves into a Society to protect his Fame, and Erected a Monument to his and your own honour in Westminster Abbey. . . . Therefore as the *Fair Sex and the Poet* have mutually admir'd and defended Each other, I shall address myself to them in particular to protect our Bard from Ev'ry Attack of those who having refin'd

---

[1] *Lloyd's Evening Post*, Sept. 15–18, 1769, **25**, 266, col. 3.
[2] *The Universal Magazine*, Sept. 1769, **45**, 158–9.
[3] Ibid.

away their Feelings must have lost their Taste for *Nature,
Beauty* and SHAKESPEARE.[1]

He then spoke his rhymed *Epilogue to the Ladies*:

> ... In *Shakespeare*'s Name I invocate the Fair!
> Whilst on my Breast their Patron Saint I wear —
> (*shews the Medal*)
> He LOV'D the Sex — ...
> If he paints female Characters, whose Crimes,
> Belie the Sex, and startle modern Times —
> He brands them Monsters, with his pow'rful Pen!
> Nay, makes them like his Witches — almost Men! ...
> When *Juliet, Hero, Imogen,* he drew,
> And sprightly *Rosalind,* he dreamt of you!
> Whate'er of *Wit,* of *Grace,* or *Fancy* flow'd,
> *Shakespeare* on *you* his best, lov'd Theme bestow'd!
> 'Twas *you* engross'd his first, his fond Regard,
> And you, to Nature just, revere the Bard — ...
> The Name of Shakespeare ever will be dear ...
> Your Daughters' Daughters shall contest his Pow'r,
> Till Language fail, or Time shall be no more;
> Shall on his Cause enraptur'd Judges sit,
> And *Beauty* ever prove, the *Patroness of Wit.*[2]

This ended the morning's entertainment,[3] and in Victor's
words:

Thus, as *Pope* says, was this *Feast of Reason, and the Flow of Soul,*
never enjoyed with more Rapture than was testified by every

---

[1] David Garrick, *M.S. Journal of Journey to France and Italy, 1763–64,*
124–6. The Folger Shakespeare Library. The speech is pasted into the
manuscript with the heading 'After King's speech'.

[2] Victor, op. cit., 3, 223–6.

[3] Mrs England, op. cit., 40–41, is of the opinion that the order of procedure
was the following: Garrick's apologetic speech, his prose address to the ladies,
'Epilogue to the Ladies' in verse, Garrick's challenge to the audience to speak
for or against Shakespeare, Mr King's speech, and as answer to that, Garrick's prose 'Oration in Honour of Shakespeare'.

Auditor! Every Friend congratulating each other on the Pleasure he had received.[1]

Garrick had conquered adverse circumstances and achieved a great success.

At four there was a public dinner at the amphitheatre, at which a turtle, weighing 150 pounds, was served, 'which with a number of other Dainties, and rich Wines, was only a proper Entertainment for the splendid Company assembled there'.[2] From five till seven o'clock the band played and the company again participated in the singing of ballads, glees, and catches, some of them not sung the day before. The following catch would certainly be popular after Garrick's acting of Falstaff in the Ode:

> *NYM, Pistol* and *Bardolph,* with merry old *Jack,*
> One morning made sport of their pupil, prince *Harry;*
> When *Falstaff* cried out for a bumper of sack,
> To *Quickly,* his hostess, and bid her not tarry;
> Ah! hah! cry'd the prince, honest boy is it so!
> The wheels of your wit, must be oil'd as they go.[3]

Other pieces were more ambitious, such as the roundelay 'Sisters of the tuneful strain' and two pieces obviously intended for performance by the band and singers only. The first of these was 'Queen Mab', a cantata (music by Dibdin and text by Bickerstaffe) with recitatives and airs; a charming trifle describing the fairies' arrival to take part in the Jubilee. The other, very different in tone, with text by Garrick, was 'The Country Girl. A Comic Serenata', likewise with recitative and airs, in which one

---

[1] Victor, op. cit., 3, 226.
[2] Ibid.
[3] *Shakespeare's Garland,* p. 18.

country girl asks another what all the to-do is about and who is being honoured — and frankly does not believe the answer:

> *All this for a Poet — O no —*
> *Who liv'd lord knows how long ago?* . . .
> *A poet, a poet, O no,*
> > *'Tis not so,* . . .
>
> *It must be some great man,*
> *A prince, or a state-man*
> *It can't be a poet — O no* . . .[1]

Again, as on the preceding day, tea and coffee were served after the entertainment.

A very elaborate and expensive display of fireworks[2] was planned for eight o'clock, to be observed from the amphitheatre and the river bank. Angelo made brave attempts at carrying through the plan, but the heavy rain, still falling, soaked the fireworks, and most of them would not go off. Henry Angelo reports that 'the fireworks were in dudgeon with the waterworks. The rockets would not ascend for fear of catching cold, and the surly crackers went out at a single pop.'[3] After this disappointment the company went to their lodgings to prepare for the masquerade, which was to begin at midnight.

Boswell had a quiet dinner with the Rosses and the Kings and later tea with the bookseller, Richard Baldwin, publisher of the *Public Advertiser*. But he left early, for he had not finished writing some verses to be spoken and distributed by himself, in the character of a Corsican

---

[1] *Shakespeare's Garland*, 24–25.

[2] For a detailed list of the fireworks, see reproduction of the Handbill, p. 104.

[3] Angelo, op. cit., I, 49.

chief, at the masquerade. As soon as he had finished the verses, he ran to Garrick, read them to him, and found him much pleased, especially with the stanza referring to himself:[1]

> Had *Shakespeare* liv'd our story to relate,
> And hold his torch o'er our unhappy fate;
> Liv'd with majestick energy to tell
> How long we fought, what heroes nobly fell!
> Had *Garrick*, who Dame Nature's pencil stole,
> Just where old SHAKESPEARE dropt it, . . .
> . . . shewn us on the tragick scene,
> With fame embalm'd our deeds of death had been;
> If from his eyes had flashed the Corsick fire,
> Men less had gaz'd to pity — than admire![2]

In his journal Boswell mentions that he found difficulty in getting the verses printed in time for the masquerade. He went to a man who advertised 'printing at an hour's notice', only to find that 'Mr. Angelo's fireworks turned his head, and made him idle. He preferred them to all poetical fire.' He then went to the regular Stratford printer, who was employing a boy of Scots extraction from Birmingham. Boswell says:

I found him a clever, active fellow, and set him to work directly. He brought me a proof to the masquerade ball about two in the morning. But could not get my verses thrown off in time for me to give them about in my Corsican dress.[3]

On account of the torrential rains the company experienced considerable difficulty in getting to the amphi-

---

[1] *Boswell in Search of a Wife*, 283.

[2] *The London Magazine*, Sept. 1769, **38**, 455–56. The French forces had only recently, in the Battle of Ponte Nuevo May 8, 1769, overwhelmed the Corsican insurgents and secured the attachment of the island to France.

[3] Boswell, op. cit., above.

theatre at midnight, when according to most accounts
the masquerade was supposed to begin, although the
handbill stated that it would start at eleven o'clock.
Henry Angelo noted:

The floods threatened to carry the mighty fabric [i.e. the building]
clean off. As it was, the horses had to wade through the meadow,
knee-deep to reach it; and planks were stretched from the
entrance to the floors of the carriages, for the company to *alight*.
Such a flood has not been witnessed there in the memory of man.[1]

But the guests managed to arrive; the room was soon
extremely crowded and nearly one thousand persons
were thought to have been present. 'All the Nobility and
the principal Gentry, who carried their own Dresses
thither, were very splendid – but those who had not that
Advantage, paid dearly for *Habits* brought by the Deal-
ers of *London*.'[2] In fact, the prices were exorbitant:

Dresses of the meanest sort were hired at Four Guineas each . . .
those, however, who could not be accommodated to their Minds
or did not choose to pay such a Sum, were admitted with Masques
only, and there were many present even without Masks the
principal Part of the Nobility were in Dominos: the literary
Gentlemen were also in Dominos – the unusual Wetness of the
Evening, and Want of proper Convenience, rendering it impossible,
or disagreeable, to take any Pains in the Assumption of fictitious
Characters.[3]

In spite of this Boswell felt:

The Masquerade Ball was one of the best that has been in Britain.
There were many rich, elegant, and curious Dresses, many
beautiful Women and some Characters well supported . . . only

[1] Angelo, op. cit., 1, 48–49.
[2] Victor, op. cit., 3, 227.
[3] *The St James Chronicle*, Sept. 9–12, 1769, 4, col. 3.

I must observe that a Masquerade is an Entertainment, which does not seem to be much suited to the Genius of the British Nation. In warmer Countries, where the People have a great Flow of Spirits, and a Readiness at Repartee, a Masquerade is exceedingly agreeable: but the Reserve and Taciturnity which is observable among us, makes us appear awkward and embarrassed in feigned Characters. Many of our Stratford Masks seemed angry when one accosted them.[1]

Of himself Boswell wrote in his journal: 'I was quite happy at the Masquerade. . . . I got acquainted with Mr. Murphy, Mr. Colman, Mr. Kelly, Mr. Foote at this Jubilee; also with . . . many others. My Corsican dress attracted everybody. I was as much a favourite as I could desire.'[2]

All accounts of the Jubilee mention him and his striking costume. In its September issue, *The London Magazine* published '*An Account of the Armed* Corsican Chief, at the Masquerade, at Shakespeare's *Jubilee* at Stratford-upon-Avon, Sept. 1769', together with a full-page plate of Boswell in the dress of a Corsican Chief (see illustration, p. 99). *The London Chronicle* reprinted the account in its issue of October 3rd–5th. It is so very detailed that it was most probably produced by Boswell himself:

. . . He wore a short dark-coloured coat of coarse cloath, scarlet breeches, and white spatter-dashes, his cap or bonnet was of black cloth; on the front of it was embroidered, in gold letters, VIVA LA LIBERTA; and on one side of it was an handsome blue feather and cockade, so that it had an elegant, as well as a warlike appearance. On the breast of his coat was sewed a Moor's head, the crest of Corsica surrounded with branches of laurel. He had also a cartridge-pouch, into which was stuck a stiletto, and on his

---

[1] *The Public Advertiser*, Sept. 16, 1769, 2, cols. 2–3.
[2] *Boswell in Search of a Wife*, 283.

left side a pistol was hung upon the belt of his cartridge-pouch. He had a fusee slung across his shoulder, wore no powder in his hair, but had it platted, at its full length, with a knot of blue ribbon at the end of it. He had by way of a staff a very curious vine . . . He wore no mask, saying that it was not proper for a gallant Corsican. . . .[1]

Besides Boswell, other distinguished characters were mentioned, such as Lady Pembroke, Mrs Bouverie, and Mrs Crewe, dressed as the three witches in *Macbeth*; Miss Nancy Ladbroke as Dame Quickly in *The Merry Wives of Windsor*; Lord Grosvenor, 'magnificently dressed in an Eastern habit', Mrs Yates, the actress, as a Petit-Maître, her husband as a waggoner, and a 'gentle-man from Oxford' as Lord Ogleby in *The Clandestine Marriage*.[2]

Apparently it took some time before the assembled company developed the gay spirit appropriate to a masquerade. Henry Angelo, being Italian by descent and therefore belonging by race to one of these peoples with 'a great Show of Spirits', describes the progress to the point where the more stolid British were at last stirred to enthusiasm. First Garrick greeted the assembly with a long and eloquent address, which made the audience yawn; and they were not even roused by the entrance of Dr Kenrick,

who by way of enlivening the scene, stalked in as Shakespeare's Ghost [he bore a strong resemblance to the portraits of Shakespeare] to see what they were all about, and shivered as though he had passed the last four and twenty hours on the cold marble. Even the fascination of Lady Pembroke, Hon. Mrs. Crewe, and Mrs. Bouverie . . . could not charm dulness from her throne;

[1] *The London Magazine*, Sept. 1769, 38, 455, 1.
[2] Ibid., 3, 107–8.

Boswell as a Corsican Chief
(from *The London Magazine*, Sept. 1769)

and though the dancing made the scene look somewhat more bright, it was not until the *beaux* and the *belles* assembled round the magnificent supper-tables, that joy lit up the scene. Then all was gaiety, and the fête proceeded gloriously.[1]

Boswell's doings at the masquerade are described in some detail:

He was first accosted by Mrs. Garrick, with whom he had a good deal of conversation. There was an admirable dialogue between Lord Grosvenor, in the character of a Turk, and the Corsican, on the different constitutions of their countries so opposite to each other — despotism and liberty — and Captain Thomson of the navy, in the character of an honest tar, kept it up very well; he expressed a strong inclination to stand by the brave islanders. Mr. Boswell danced both a minuet and a country dance with a very pretty Irish lady, Mrs. Sheldon . . . she was dressed in a genteel domino, and before she danced, threw off her mask.[2]

When the proofs of his '*Verses* in the Character of a *Corsican* at SHAKESPEARE's Jubilee, At Stratford-upon-Avon, Sept. 6, 1769' were brought to him at two o'clock, he tried to read the poem to the company, but 'the crowd would not suspend its diversions to hear him', though he had the consolation of seeing his broadside reprinted a few days later in *Lloyd's Evening Post* (September the 10th), *The London Chronicle* (September the 10th–12th) and in the September issues of many magazines. Nevertheless, Boswell thoroughly enjoyed himself all evening. Dibdin, always pessimistic, commented: 'I hardly see how he could have been in a good humour, for I saw him at the masquerade dancing with the water over his shoes.'[3]

---

[1] Angelo, op. cit., I, 49–50.

[2] 'An Account of an Armed Corsican Chief' in *The London Magazine*, Sept. 1769, 38, 455, 1–2.

[3] Dibdin, op. cit., I, 78.

Samuel Foote appeared as 'The Devil on Two Sticks', a character part he had performed, to great applause, at the Little Theatre in the Haymarket. The sticks at least were not assumed for this occasion; as the result of a silly practical joke he had been thrown from an unruly horse, had broken both his legs, and been forced since then to walk with two sticks. At the masquerade some found him 'singularly unpleasant'. Another, more used to his sarcastic tone, remarked: 'Mr. Foote indulged in the sallies of wit which seemed to please all by sparing none.'[1] His biographer described Foote's way of enjoying himself at the Jubilee:

Foote . . . cared little for the bard, he came simply with the one motive – that of plaguing Garrick . . . [He came] down *not* to help, but to *annoy*. His companion was Murphy, and the ill-natured pair went about prying into everything, laughing at everything, and disheartening poor Garrick as much as they could . . . But Foote did not succeed in ruffling the actor's sweet temper, or in making him depart from the rule of restraint . . . Foote did not wait to see the close of the festivities [he left that night] and returned to town well primed with all the absurdities he had seen.[2]

Another visitor wrote an amusing account of the masquerade to *The Gentleman's Magazine*:

. . . at twelve began the masquerade. My dress consisted of——, a silver medal of Shakespeare, pendant from a skye-blue ribbon around my neck, and a cockade of rainbow-coloured ribbon in my hat: not a bad figure you will say: and I assure you that I was well entertained. The characters which were mistaken, afforded me as much or more diversion than those that were kept up; and many of them indeed would have been really as well filled, if they had been

[1] Davies, op. cit., 4, 217.
[2] Percy H. Fitzgerald, *Samuel Foote, a biography*, London 1910, 301-2.

filled with straw. – Surely a masquerade taxes the abilities of mankind in general too high. But one sailor out of six could dance a hornpipe, and but one more box his compass. – But one Oxford scholar could speak Greek; and not one told me readily his name and college. Not one conjurer informed me whether he could tell my fortune best by chiromancy or catoptromancy. None of four farmers knew 'how a score of ewes sold now'; and the harlequin was stiff as a poker. – Two Slenders did I drive around the room because they had no simple . . . An excellent Lord Ogleby and a jockey, and as good a Dutch skipper, and a devil, and many of the fancied dresses were truly splendid and elegant. . . . I had much conversation with the three weird sisters, before I found out that their masks hid the three handsomest faces in England, Mrs. Crewe, Mrs. Bouverie, and Mrs. Payne, – I enjoyed the night prodigiously, danced a dance or two masked, and retired satisfied and unfatigued between six and seven.[1]

Cradock comments on the departure from the amphitheatre; like the entry, it was somewhat unceremonious:

. . . all zealous friends endeavoured to keep up the spirit of it as long as they could; till they were at last informed that the Avon was rising so very fast, that no delay could be admitted. The ladies of our party were conveyed by planks from the building to the footsteps of the coach, and we found that the wheels had been two feet deep in water from the rapid inundation.[2]

Thus ended the second day.

3. THE THIRD DAY – DEPARTURE FROM STRATFORD

It had rained heavily all through the night between Thursday and Friday and the rain was still pouring down at midday and continued into the afternoon. The usual public breakfast was held in the Town Hall. The

---

[1] *The Gentleman's Magazine*, Sept. 1769, 39, 423.
[2] Cradock, op. cit., I, 218–19.

Jubilee race was run as scheduled at noon, in spite of the weather; the beautiful race-course was partly flooded and the horses splashed through the race knee-deep in water. All five entries started (see the handbill, p. 104). Mr Pratt, a groom, rode his own brown colt, Whirligig, to victory, and received the valuable prize of a silver cup, engraved with Shakespeare's arms, and worth £50. Afterwards he 'declared his Resolution never to part with it, though he honestly confessed – he knew very little about *Plays*, or Master SHAKESPEARE'.[1]

Garrick had been requested to repeat his Ode on Friday, but was prevented from doing so by the flooding of the amphitheatre, nor could the postponed procession be held because of the continuing bad weather. Thus, to Garrick's great disappointment, the entertainment that was to form the most spectacular and elaborate part of his plan never took place in Stratford.

No common dinner was held that day; people ate at their lodgings or at the White Lion Inn. But some may have braved the floods at the amphitheatre, for Victor mentions that

At their Return from the Race, the Company repaired to the AMPHITHEATRE to Dinner – the French Horns and the Clarinets attending – from there to their lodgings to dress for the Ball at night.[2]

He could be mistaken, if he did not go himself and wrote only from hearsay. Nobody else mentions this, and judging from the state of the building when Cradock left it about five o'clock in the morning, it could not have been usable.

As soon as it was known that no pageant would be

---

[1] Victor, op. cit., 3, 229. [2] Ibid., 3, 230.

Shakeſpeare's Jubilee.

Wedneſday, SEPTEMBER 6th.

FIRST DAY.

Began at 6 o'Clock in the Morning, with a grand Diſcharge of Cannon, ringing of Bells, &c. At Seven, o'Clock a Grand Seranade conſiſting of Guittars, German Flutes, &c. accompanied with ſeveral good Voices. At Nine o'CLOCK, was a PUBLIC BREAKFAST at the TOWN-HALL; During which, the Drums of the *Warwickſhire Militia,* beat ſeveral fine Marches, accompanied by the Fifes.

From thence they proceeded to the CHURCH to hear

The ORATORIO of *JUDITH,*

Which began exactly at ELEVEN.

From Church there was a full CHORUS of VOCAL and INSTRUMENTAL MUSIC to the AMPHITHEATRE; where, at Three o'Clock, was

An ORDINARY for Gentlemen and Ladies.

About Five o'Clock, a Collection of NEW SONGS, BALLADS, ROUNDELAYS, CATCHES, GLEES, &c. was performed in the AMPHITHEATRE; after which was a BALL, which began at Nine, with NEW MINUETS, (compoſed for the Occaſion) and played by the whole Band.

SECOND DAY

Was a PUBLIC BREAKFAST, at Nine o'Clock, accompanied as before; from thence they proceeded to the Amphitheatre, where

AN ODE

(Upon Dedicating a BUILDING and Erecting a STATUE to the Memory of *SHAKESPEARE*) was performed.

This Day was to have been a PAGEANT of the principal Characters in the inimitable Plays wrote by the Immortal *Shakeſpeare,* but the Weather being bad was obliged to be omitted.

At Four An Ordinary for Ladies and Gentlemen.

At Eight, The following FIREWORKS:

FIRST FIRING.

No.
1 Twelve Half-pound Sky Rockets.
2 Four Tourbillons.
3 Two Vertical Wheels, illuminated.
4 Two Caſcades, with Reports; one Fir Tree, in Chineſe Fire.
5 Two regulating Pieces of three Mutations each; viz. Sun and Stars; Porcupine's Quills; and, large double Stars of eight Points.
6 Two Pidgeon Wheels, with ſeven Pidgeons each.
7 Two Horizontal Tables, with ſix Vertical Wheels and Globes illuminated.

SECOND FIRING.

8 Twelve Pound Sky Rockets.
9 Four Tourbillons.
10 Two regulating Pieces of three Mutations: 1ſt, Brilliant Wheels with yellow and blue Lights. 2d, A brilliant Sun. 3d, A brilliant Star with eight Points.
11 Two Diamond Pieces of Stars and Fountains, to finiſh with Mines.

No.
12 Two Pyramids of twenty-one Chineſe Fires and Boxes, each.
13 Two new Pieces of changeable Fires, interſecting each other.

THIRD FIRING.

14 Twelve Pound Sky Rockets, with Flames, Tails, Stars, &c.
15 Four Tourbillons.
16 Two large horizontal Wheels, changing into a vertical Sun illuminated.
17 Two Figure Pieces, containing ſixteen Poriſonies of brilliant Fires, and vertical Wheels in the Centre, with yellow Fires.
18 Two regulating Pieces of three Mutations each, viz. A large Wheel, illuminated; two brilliant Suns; ſix Branches of new Fires, repreſenting Ears of Corn.
19 Two Pieces called the Fort, conſiſting of brilliant Fountains, Roman Candles, and Chineſe Jurbs, with Reports.

And at Eleven the MASQUERADE, the moſt brilliant ever ſeen.

THIRD DAY.

At Twelve o'Clock, a Race for a *Jubilee Cup,* of 50l. Value, for which the following Horſes ſtarted:

Mr. *Pratt's* Brown Colt, *Whirligig,* J. *Pratt,* Blue · · · · 4	1	1
Hon. Mr. *King's* Bay Colt, Name unknown, T. *Camel,* White 1	4	4
Lord *Grofvenor's* Colt, *Scholes* · · · · · · · 2	3	3
Mr. *Fettiplace's* Bay Colt, *Pompillion,* E. *Freeman,* Green · 3	2	5
Mr. *Watſon's* Grey Colt, *Lofty,* John *Rider,* Red. · · · · 5	5	2

At Nine o'Clock the following Fireworks, which, thro' the badneſs of the Weather, could not be let off the Night before, viz.

1 Four Balloons.
2 Four Air Balloons.
3 Four Tourbillons.
4 Two Figure Pieces, conſiſting of five vertical Wheels and Spiral Wheels, illuminated.
5 One Figure Piece, conſiſting of five vertical Wheels, &c. four Spiral Wheels, illuminated.

7 Twelve large Chineſe Jurbs.
8 Four Dozen of Water-Rockets.
9 Twelve Mortars with Air Balloons, illuminated.
10 One large Sun on the Top of a tranſparent and illuminated Building, with ſix Pots d'Aigrous, &c. and a Flight of ſix Dozen Half-Pound Sky Rockets.

And, at Eleven, by the Requeſt of the LADIES, was a BALL, at the HALL, now call'd SHAKESPARE's-HALL.

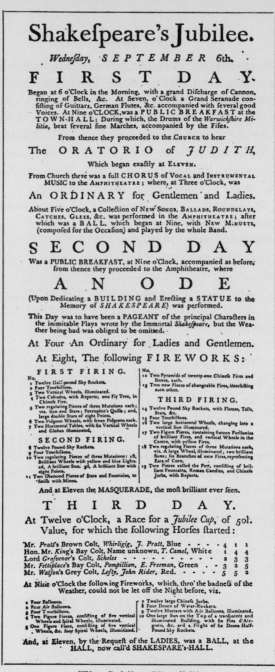

The Jubilee Handbill
(from the copy in *The British Museum*)

held, 'the principal Part of the Company, who had carriages of their own, went out of Town'.[1] Boswell did not get home from the masquerade till past six in the morning. He slept for about three hours and then went to call at Mr Baldwin's, where he had breakfast. He writes in his journal:

After the joy of the Jubilee came the uneasy reflection that I was in a little village in wet weather and knew not how to get away, for all the post-chaises were bespoke, I don't know how many times, by different companies. We were like a crowd in a theatre. It was impossible we could all go at a time.[2]

He was offered a seat in a post-chaise for the next morning by 'a man of Scots extraction', and accepted. Whereupon he went to the White Lion, and was recognized there by two Lichfield men, who knew Dr Johnson well, and asked him to join them for dinner. He began to think that his companion for the post-chaise, 'who seemed to be very dissipated', would not be a good travelling companion. So when he had tea later with the printer William Richardson and a Captain Johnson of an Indiaman and they offered him a seat in their coach, he was glad to accept the offer. He then called on Garrick and gave him a copy of his 'Verses'. Garrick read them to him in such a manner that he was quite elated. 'They seemed admirable.' But he had another reason for visiting Garrick; he had run out of money and wanted to borrow five guineas. Garrick 'told him that his brother George had taken almost all he had from him', but when Boswell insisted that he had to have the money, Garrick went to his wife and got it from her.[3]

[1] *The St James Chronicle*, Sept. 9–12, 1769, 4, col. 2.
[2] *Boswell in Search of a Wife*, 283.
[3] Ibid., 283–5.

Meanwhile the rain had stopped, so fireworks became possible. They were announced in the handbill:

At nine o'clock the following Fireworks, which, thro' the badness of the Weather, could not be let off the Night before, viz.

1. Four Balloons.
2. Four Air Balloons.
3. Four Tourbillons.
4. Two figure pieces, consisting of five vertical Wheels and spiral Wheels, illuminated.
5. One Figure Piece, consisting of five vertical Wheels, etc., four Spiral Wheels, illuminated
7. [*sic*] Twelve large Chinese Jurbs.
8. Four Dozen of Water-Rockets.
9. Twelve Mortars with Air Balloons, illuminated.
10. One large Sun on the Top of a transparent and illuminated Building, with six Pots d'Airgretts, etc. and a Flight of six Dozen Half-Pound Sky Rockets.[1]

Victor remarks:

This evening (being fair weather) there was a grand FIREWORK play'd off before the AMPHITHEATRE — which closed the most splendid JUBILEE that ever was *plan'd* or *executed* in ENGLAND.[2]

It was not, in fact, quite the end, for at the request of the remaining ladies an Assembly was held at eleven o'clock in the Town Hall, at which 'Mrs. Garrick danced a Minuet beyond description gracefully, and joined in the Country Dances, which ended at Four, and put an end to the Jubilee'.[3]

---

[1] See *Handbill*, p. 104.
[2] Victor, op. cit., 3, 230.
[3] *The St James Chronicle*, Sept. 9–12, 1769, 4, col. 2.

On Saturday morning, September the 9th,

. . . the Want of Carriages occasioned a more general Confusion, than any antecedent Circumstance; every body wanted to quit Stratford, but few, unless those who were down with their own Carriages, could attempt it; Five Guineas; but Five, nay Fifty Guineas were unable to attain it.[1]

The Host of the White Lion Inn thought it would take about three weeks before all the guests could leave, and was glad at the prospect of earning more money.

After leaving a note for the dissipated Scot, informing him that he had to leave very early, Boswell set out with his two travelling companions at 5 a.m. Their chaise was in bad condition and had to be left in Oxford for repairs. They spent the night there and set out in another chaise on Sunday morning, stopped at Salthill for dinner, where they met Colman and Lacy, and reached London on Sunday night.[2]

Garrick, staying in Stratford for another day, arrived at his country home, Hampton House, on Monday September the 11th.[3]

[1] *The St James Chronicle*, Sept. 9–12, 1769, 4, col. 2.
[2] *Boswell in Search of a Wife*, 285–6.
[3] *The St James Chronicle*, Sept. 12–14, 1769, 1, col. 1.

III

Public Reactions to the Jubilee

Enormous public interest was aroused by the Stratford Jubilee. The newspapers and magazines were full of accounts and comments both favourable and adverse. The Ode was widely written about and both praised and severely criticized. Several theatrical pieces either describing or referring to the Jubilee were hastily written, and some of these give a good idea of contemporary reactions to the event. These are not to be confused with Colman's elaborate piece that attempted to anticipate or rival Garrick's own triumphant Drury Lane production, which will be described in our next chapter. In the present one we are concerned only with the immediate repercussions.

Upon their return to London many visitors were highly critical of the Jubilee and wrote letters of complaint to the newspapers and magazines. They mentioned the inadequate arrangements, the overcrowding, the poor accommodation, the hostile attitude towards the visitors on the part of the common inhabitants of Stratford, the lack of conveyances, the poor and insufficient food, and last, but not least, the exorbitant prices charged for everything. They thought also that some provisions should have been made against possible bad weather, so that the principal plans could have been carried out and not just cancelled. Some of their

grumbling was no doubt caused by the misery and dis-
comfort suffered by most of the guests during the period
of bad weather; many of their complaints were
certainly justified.

A letter-writer, signing himself 'Musidorus', gives
shocking instances of the high prices charged:

Half a guinea has been charged for the standing of a single horse
without either hay or oats, and Mr. Foote, who, by-the-bye, paid
nine guineas for six hours sleep, was charged two shillings for being
told what it was o'clock. . . . This however was nothing to what
another writer was asked for the use of a greatcoat – the demand
was only half a guinea. . . . A gentleman had nine pence inserted
in his bill for washing a pocket handkerchief. . . .

At an ordinary in the Amphitheatre, which was furnished and
most miserably furnished, from the White Lyon, we paid eighteen
shillings for our dinner and wine. We indeed had something which
was called Turtle, and something under the denomination of
Claret; but if it had not been for the dignity of the appellations we
might as well have regaled upon neck of beef, and Southampton
Port – Impositions of this nature we should easily have overlooked,
had our beds been anyway tolerable . . . but the most wretched
shed in the town that had a few rags patched into a bed, was
estimated at one guinea a night . . . an eminent actor was charged
a shilling every time he repaired to *the Temple of the Graces* at a
particular Inn and that — were rated at eighteen pence for the
use of the same convenience, who did not lodge in the house. The
inhabitants of the town were determined to make us pay for our
Jubilee . . . we never could have a chicken above half plucked and
I am at this moment almost choked with the stubble of my pro-
vender, for butcher's meat was scarcely comeatable on any consideration.

After this he comments on the fear and resentment
shown by the common inhabitants, in spite of all the

good money they were earning, and goes on to estimate that the profit on the sale of jubilee ribands must have amounted to about a thousand pounds and on the jubilee medals to at least three thousand. He believes that the total cost of the Jubilee must have been about fifty thousand pounds. The damage done by the heavy rains was great.

The amphitheatre, which is now above a foot deep in water, from the heavy rains and its low situation on the border of the Avon will be useless [a great loss to the Corporation that had paid for its erection] . . . the great rains, which several people consider as a judgment on our poetical idolatry, were a material prejudice to our entertainment; they prevented the theatrical procession and prevented Mr. Garrick from reciting his ode the second time. Besides this they spoiled our firework, our masquerade and our race – yet after all the expence, fatigue and disappointment I candidly acknowledge that we were overpaid by the single recitation of the ode. This part of the Jubilee was so thoroughly admirable and gave so perfect a satisfaction, that I should not hesitate at another Stratford expedition to hear it, and I am satisfied that the majority of the company are entirely of my sentiment.[1]

Thus he ends his letter with some praise; for that matter so does Boswell, though his attitude towards the high prices is that of a wealthy man:

Much noise has been made about the high Price of every Thing at Stratford. I own that I cannot agree that such Censures are just: it was reasonable that Shakespeare's Townsmen should partake of the Jubilee as well as we Strangers did; they as a Jubilee of Profit, we of Pleasure. As it lasted but for a few Nights, a Guinea a Night for a Bed was not an Imposition. Nobody was understood to come there who had not plenty of Money.

[1] *The London Chronicle*, Sept. 12–14, 1769, **26**, 263, 2–3.

But Boswell himself ran short of money before he left and had to borrow from Garrick. He mentions the inconveniences and the bad tempers of the last day and continues:

I laughed away Spleen by a droll Simile: Taking the Whole of this Jubilee, said I, is like eating an Artichoke entire. We have some fine Mouthfuls, but also swallow the Leaves and the Hair, which are confoundedly difficult of Digestion. After all, however, I am highly satisfied with my Artichoke.

To conclude as I began – I will always be of the Opinion that Shakespeare's Jubilee at Stratford upon Avon is an Institution which does Honour not only to our immortal Bard, but to all who have contributed towards it; and I hope that every seven Years it shall be celebrated with equal Ardour of Enthusiasm as it has been in 1769.[1]

So like 'Musidorus' he ends on a cheerful note. Some weeks later another correspondent uses the most scathing terms about the inhabitants of Stratford:

The low People of Stratford upon Avon are without doubt as ignorant as any in the whole Island. I could not possibly imagine that there were such Beings in the most remote, and least frequented Parts of the Kingdom. I talked with many, particularly the old People, and not one of them but was frightened at the Preparations for the Jubilee, and did not know what they were about. Many of them thought that Mr. G — would raise Devils, and fly in a Chariot about the Town. They ordered those whom they had Power over, not to stir out the Day of the Jubilee; and when the Cannon came, they would have it that some Mischief was going forward about the Pretender.

It is impossible to describe their Absurdity; and indeed Providence seems by producing Shakespeare and the rest of his Townsmen, to shew the two Extremes of Human Nature.[2]

[1] *The Public Advertiser*, Sept. 16, 1769, 2, col. 3.
[2] *The St James Chronicle*, Oct. 12, 1769, 4, col. 1.

Benjamin Victor also comments on

. . . the scandalous Behaviour of the very *low People* of the Town
of *Stratford*, in regard to their *Avarice*, and shameful Extortions;
as well as their absurd Notions relating to the Jubilee. They looked
upon *Mr. Garrick* as a *Magician*, who could and would raise the
Devil! . . . They were confirmed in their Absurdities by the
black Looks and secret Operations of those who were employed in
making the *Fireworks* and looked on the heavy Rains that fell
during the Jubilee as a Mark of Heaven's Anger. In short their
Desire to get Money, and the Terrors lest they should deal with
the Devil, occasioned great Mirth to many of the Neighbours and
Gentlemen who delight in Humour and Pleasantry.[1]

There were complaints about the kind of entertainment
offered; one angry visitor condemns it as being in bad
taste (the only exception being the recitation of the ode).
He writes as follows:

Oratorio, Balls, Masquerade, Fireworks, they were such, as
common occasions might produce, well enough calculated for
vacant minds, to gratify ostentatious pride, juvenile vanity and
luxurious opulence, and in short, such as policy directed, in
compliance with the vitiated taste of these times, to engage and
retain the company.[2]

Severe criticism is voiced in a letter, signed A JUBILITE,
to *The Town and Country Magazine*:

Sir,

    It was surprising to me that your shrewd correspondent from
Amen Corner, should not have classed the Jubilee at Stratford
upon Avon among the political and m — l humbugs of the present
aera. To draw a number of people so many miles, and at such

---

[1] Victor, op. cit., 3, 231–2.
[2] *Lloyd's Evening Post*, Sept. 15–18, 1769, 25, 266, 2.

expence, under a pretext of giving a diversion that was to gratify every taste, and please every palate — and then produce such a paultry amusement, omitting the most capital articles in the bill of fare, is certainly such an insult to the understanding of the public, as they cannot tamely put up with. . . . A scarcity of provisions, a want of conveyances, or even covering from the inclemency of the weather, a rotunda that was not waterproof, and masquerade dresses at five guineas a-piece, form a pretty collection of omissions and impositions. If it should be pleaded that the fireworks could not be played off on account on the inclemency of the weather, the same excuse cannot be urged with any degree of propriety for the procession not taking place, and the crowning of Shakespeare being laid aside; as the managers of this jubilee of jubilees should have prepared against such accidents, by an awning or covering of some sort, which might have been procured at a small expence, and not only facilitated the representation of these parts of the entertainment, but also secured the company from rain. . . .

That you may not think that I complain without reason, judge if my diversion was adequate to the following expence: [here he gives a detailed list of his expenses for the whole trip. They total £49. 2. 0.]. Such, Sir, was the tax imposed for this extraordinary Jubilee, which has been very pertinently defined by the good-natured Devil upon Two Sticks in the Hay-Market.

He ends his letter by quoting the 'Devil's definition in full:

A Jubilee, as it hath lately appeared, is a public invitation urged by puffing, to go post without horses, to an obscure borough without representatives, governed by a mayor and aldermen who are no magistrates, to celebrate a great poet whose own works have made him immortal by an ode without poetry, music without harmony, dinners without victuals and lodging without beds, a masquerade where half the people appear bare-faced, a horse-race up to the knees in water, fireworks extinguished as soon as they were lighted, and a gingerbread amphitheatre which, like a house of cards, tumbled to pieces as soon as it was finished.[1]

This definition was Foote's parting shot in his campaign against the Jubilee and its Steward, written immediately upon his return to London and the summer theatre in the Haymarket. He had kept Garrick on tenterhooks for months with his threats of ridicule: first of producing a mock-ode, next a mock-jubilee at the Haymarket to coincide with the Stratford Jubilee and last a mock-theatrical procession. Fortunately for Garrick none of these threats materialized, and although Foote went about Stratford making highly sarcastic remarks and was rather offensive as 'The Devil on Two Sticks' at the masquerade, he did not disturb or upset the proceedings as had been much feared. There was no open break with Garrick, who must have drawn a sigh of relief when Foote left Stratford immediately after the masquerade. Clearly their mutual friends had persuaded Foote not to be too provocative.[2] His audiences at the Haymarket were amused by his sarcastic and apt definition 'so dexterously managed, that the Persons themselves who are the Object of his Pleasantry cannot help joining in the full Chorus of Laughter',[3] and even Garrick himself laughed at it and used part of it in his production of *The Jubilee* at Drury Lane. It was freely quoted in London and printed in various newspapers and magazines.

It did, however, call forth a humorous letter of protest from Stratford, dated September the 30th, in defence of the reputation of that town:

[1] *The Town and Country Magazine*, Sept. 1769, 1, 477.
[2] For further details see England, op. cit., 11–14.
[3] Victor, op. cit., 3, 192–3.

To the celebrated Devil of the Haymarket
My dear Asmodeus,

Your Description of our late Stratford Jubilee . . . convinces me of how merry a Disposition you are, and that nothing is likely to alter it, till you *visit the infernal Regions again.*

Your *Account* (give the Devil his due) is in many Instances *sufficiently laughable*; but who, except yourself, could have made such *Mistakes* and *Blunders* as you have done, not without some *Reproach,* my dear Friend, to your funny Reputation.

If our Visiters, 'came post to us (as you say) without Horses'; they certainly made use of Moore's Machines, or flew upon Broomsticks through the Air, in the Manner you yourself did; and therefore *you,* of *all* Conjurers should by no Means have blamed them for it: Perhaps Shakespeare himself would have seemed it an Impropriety, if they had used any other Way of Conveyance.

That we had 'Dinners without Victuals' is rather — a downright — Mistake: But that some of the Food was such as Asmodeus himself would scarce eat, is true enough; however, for this Mr. Devil, you may thank yourself; knowing that, *whoever* sent us the Meat; *you* and *your Tribe* sent us *the Cooks*! You have found grievous Fault with *the Ode,* and with *the Musick,* though both were allowed to be *excellent*; but *this,* indeed, we all expected from you, knowing the Devil to be *an utter Enemy to all true Harmony.* You discovered also some of the same *Malignancy,* if not *Impotence,* in that you who naturally must delight in *Fire-Works,* would not, or could not, when they were extinguished, stretch out one glowing Claw to kindle them again: This shews how willing your Devilship is, Things should appear in a bad *Light* or rather *no Light at all*; . . .

If Asmodeus has any acquaintance with Mr. F —, he will do well to tell him, that his late joke of throwing away Two Shillings at the Jubilee, to know the Time of Day, is founded on a Misrepresentation, and therefore has lost its Poignancy; the Person who received the Money of him, being no Inhabitant of Stratford,

I

being one of the numerous indigent Hair-Cutters who rushed in Swarms out of London for a little Jubilean Employment, and are now returned to the Metropolis, to feast again on their usual diet of Tripe, Cow-Heels, and Sheep's Trotters.

For the instant he is reading this, and no longer, I am

Asmodeus's humble servant,

A STRATFORDIAN.[1]

As mentioned above, *The Dedication Ode* and *Shakespeare's Garland* had been published before the Jubilee and were for sale there. Now after the Jubilee the Ode and many of the best songs and ballads were reprinted in a number of newspapers and magazines.[2] The mood approaching ecstasy which had led to the extravagant praise lavished on Garrick and his presentation of the Ode at Stratford was now followed by a more sober attitude with some attempts at literary criticism.

In the 'Advertisement' prefixed to the 1769 edition of the Ode, Garrick's futile attempts to have 'some gentleman of approved ability' write the Ode are mentioned but,

. . . the lot having unluckily fallen on the person perhaps the least qualified to succeed in the attempt, it is hoped that the candour of the public will esteem the performance rather as an act of duty, than vanity in the author.

The recent attacks on Shakespeare are mentioned and the reading of a recently published anonymous work, *An Essay on the Writings and Genius of Shakespeare*, is recom-

---

[1] *The St James Chronicle*, Oct. 21–24, 1769, 2, cols. 1–2.

[2] e.g. *The St James Chronicle*, Sept. 5–7, 1769, 2, cols. 1–3; *Lloyd's Evening Post*, Sept. 9, 1769, **25**, 242–3; *The London Chronicle*, Sept. 7–9, 1769, **26**, 245–6; *The Town and Country Magazine*, Sept. 1769, **1**, 483–90, *The Scots Magazine*, Sept. 1769, **31**, 480–2; *The Annual Register*, 1769, 245–52, and many others.

mended, for it maintains 'that *England* may justly boast
the honour of producing the greatest dramatic genius in
the world!' The Advertisement continues:

To strengthen and justify the general admiration of this astonish-
ing Genius, it has been thought proper to subjoin to the Ode some
undeniable Testimonies (both in verse and prose) of his unequalled
original talents.[1]

The list of testimonies following the Ode is impressive;
there are quotations, often well chosen, from fourteen
poets, including Ben Jonson, Milton, Dryden, Pope,
Thompson, and Dr Johnson, and also Warton, Seward,
Akenside, Gray, Mason, Churchill, Jago, and the poet-
laureate William Whitehead (pp. 19–26). Then follows
a justification for the inclusion of the opinions of critics:

Though there are many, many more poets who have spoken of
SHAKESPEARE with equal praise and admiration, yet these, which
first occurred, were thought sufficient – Lest any of our readers
should think with a certain gentleman, who upon hearing Milton's
verses in praise of SHAKESPEARE, said, *He* never regarded what
was said in poetry, that the very nature of it was fiction, and had
no value about it, – there is added some undeniable testimonies
in prose, of SHAKESPEARE's unparalleled genius. (p. 26.)

Eighteen critical statements of varying lengths are then
chosen from the following authors: Dryden, Addison,
Rowe, Pope, Voltaire, Theobald, Hanmer, Lyttelton,
Warburton, Dodd, Johnson, Steevens, Capell, Hurd,
a correspondent to *Grays Inn Journal*, Colman, Walpole,
and the anonymous author of *An Essay on the Writings*

---

[1] Garrick, op. cit., see p. 71 fn. 4. The 'Advertisement' is unpaged.

and Genius of Shakespeare (pp. 26–34). Wicked tongues
hinted that all these testimonies were added so that the
booklet would be large enough to sell for one shilling and
sixpence instead of one shilling.[1] The Advertisement
ends with the following appeal and challenge:

If it shall be found, that *speaking* that part of the Ode, which has
usually been conveyed in recitative, produces a better effect, the
Author flatters himself, he may lay claim to some little merit on
that account: As to the Ode itself, he presents it to the public as an
object of their good-nature, – to his friends as an exercise of their
partiality, – to his enemies as a lucky opportunity of venting their
wit, humour, criticism, spleen, or whatever else they please, should
they think it worthy of their notice.[2]

The critics, friendly or hostile, eagerly accepted his challenge and wrote reviews of the Ode for the magazines
and newspapers. Most of them agree in praising Garrick's innovation of speaking the recitative parts as being
eminently suited to his powers of elocution. Some of
them do not think that it is fair to judge the Ode according to strict literary principles; the following statements
reveal their attitudes:

This ode though not intended as a mere vehicle for music, should
not be brought to the test of severe criticism, as a literary performance intended for the dispassionate leisure of the closet. The
author . . . is known to be pecularly happy in catching and improving hints from local and temporary circumstances; and, perhaps,
the ode before us is the greatest example of this rare felicity that
he ever gave: so that, taking it for all in all it may be the best that
could possibly have been produced upon the occasion.[3]

---

[1] Anti-Gnatho (William Kenrick?) in *The Public Advertiser*, Sept. 16,
1769, 2, col. 4.

[2] Garrick, op. cit., preceding the Ode, unpaged.

[3] *The Monthly Review*, Sept. 1769, 41, 234.

Samuel Foote

(Oil painting in the possession of the Garrick Club)

The Procession at Stratford (as it should have been)

(from the *Oxford Magazine*, Sept. and Oct. 1769)

Its great merit is its being adapted to the time, the occasion, and the speaker, so as perhaps it could not have been adapted by any other person. No composition certainly can be adapted to the elocution of another, so perfectly as the writer can adapt it to his own; . . . To examine such a piece as this by the severe rules of literary criticism, would be at once injurious and absurd: It was written for a particular purpose, and that purpose it has perfectly answered.[1]

Mr. Garrick, the author of the ode before us, speaks so modestly of his own performance, that it would seem ill-natured and invidious to bring it to the test of Horatian criticism. It would be even malicious, and betray a want of taste, to deny, that it contains several beautiful strokes of poetry.[2]

The critics then discuss passages that have given one or more of them pleasure; one writes:

One instance of the author's skill appears in the beginning of this performance. Shakespeare is not mentioned till the 30th verse, yet every preceding line contributes to his being there named with advantage. . . . The repetition of the name so long deferred, and the immediate joining in of other voices and music, produced the effect he intended, and ratified his utmost hope.[3]

Another terms the first air 'Sweetest bard that ever sung' 'by no means unpoetical, and the turns at the end is [*sic*] pleasing, even without the music',[4] whereas yet another critic goes into raptures about it:

The words of the first air, breathe nature itself; and the lines which follow, are not only incomparably beautiful, but the thought we believe is original.[5]

[1] *The Gentleman's Magazine*, Sept. 1769, **39**, 446–7.
[2] *The Critical Review*, Sept. 1769, **28**, 232.
[3] *The Monthly Review*, Sept. 1769, **41**, 234–5.
[4] *The Gentleman's Magazine*, Sept. 1769, **39**, 446.
[5] *The Critical Review*, Sept. 1769, **28**, 232.

They are favourably impressed by the passage in which Garrick compares Shakespeare to Alexander, 'Philip's fam'd unconquer'd son', and they find the part dealing with Shakespeare's comic powers and the birth of Falstaff excellent:

> . . . in this instance, he [Garrick] has almost rivalled the humour of the great master he celebrates.
>
> His representation of the birth of Falstaff from the brain of Shakespeare; his calling him first a Mountain, as a contrast to the Mouse which a Mountain was said to bring forth, and then a World, and his illustration, by observing that Falstaff and the world are both of them *round* and *wicked*, would do honour to any imagination.[1]

> The similitude of Falstaff to the world in being *wicked* and *round*, is a sally of fancy that would have been distinguished in any composition, that with propriety could have admitted it.[2]

Some critics, however, severely condemned the passage dealing with Shakespeare's command over the tragic passions (see pp. 73–74). One of them states:

> . . . the Author . . . attributed to all the passions what could be proper and true only with respect to some; . . . the passions which should have been exhibited on this occasion, are those which the poet *excites*, rather than those he *represents*. *Raging* is a fit word to signify the excess of jealousy, hatred, or indignation; but not of pity, or sorrow, or love: as these passions cannot with propriety be said to *rage*, much less can they with propriety be said to *foam*. The passions which Shakespeare *commands* are principally terror and pity, and these should not have been confounded, by an indiscriminate imputation of the same attributes. . . .
>
> In the next stanza Shakespeare is represented as a *magician*, fired by *charms*, and *spells*, and *incantations*, but there is some in-

[1] *The Monthly Review*, Sept. 1769, **41**, 236.
[2] *The Gentleman's Magazine*, Sept. 1769, **39**, 447.

congruity in this image: A magician is not the *subject* of charms, and spells, and incantations, but the *agent* that employs them.[1]

Another critic commenting on the same passage writes:

In these lines are more than one gross absurdity: *Notwithstanding* the passions were *unchained*, Shakespeare turned their *career*; and notwithstanding they were *raging*, he could *inflame* them; which implies, that if they had been chained, they might have taken a career: and that it *was difficult to inflame them*, in proportion as they were *inflamed* already. It implies also, that *all* the passions *rage* and *foam*; but perhaps a more incongruous image than *foaming pity* cannot be conceived; yet pity is one of the two passions to which tragedy is addressed; and perhaps the principal, it is both more lasting and more pleasing than terror.

These and other faults will however be easily forgiven, on the present occasion, and there is even merit in the ardour that produces them.[2]

But before these reviews appeared, a regular newspaper feud had started between Garrick's enemies and friends. It began with a very long letter to the *Public Advertiser* of September the 16th, in which the Jubilee Ode is heavily ridiculed. It was addressed to Garrick and signed Anti-Gnatho. There is some reason to believe that the author was William Kenrick.[3] He accomplishes his purpose by the use of very heavy sarcasm, calling Garrick 'The Prince of Poets', quoting some of the worse passages of the ode and then lavishing the most extravagant and fulsome praise upon them, so that they appear utterly ridiculous. A few examples follow:

[1] *The Monthly Review*, Sept. 1769, **41**, 235–6.
[2] *The Gentleman's Magazine*, Sept. 1769, **39**, 447.
[3] See Frederick A. Pottle, *The Literary Career of James Boswell Esq.*, Oxford 1929, 257–8, for the details of the whole feud.

'Do not your sympathetic Hearts accord,
'To own the Bosom's Lord?
' 'Tis he! 'Tis he!'

Inimitable! – How harmonious is the second Line! How divine
the Irruption of the third! . . .

'Prepare! Prepare! Prepare! . . .
'And Fame, expanding all her Wings,
'With all her Trumpet-Tongues proclaims,
'Shakespeare! Shakespeare! Shakespeare!'

This Passage, like the Firing of Cannon in Handel's divine
Oratorio, stuns with it's Magnificence. What a beautiful Figure
is the Tongue of Fame turned into a brazen Trumpet! And what
a happy harmonious Effect has the placing of the Accent on the
last Syllable of the Name *Shakespeare*! . . .

'What Nature had disjoin'd
'The Poet's Power combin'd
'Madness and Age, Ingratitude and Child.'

Wonderful! Wonderful indeed! That Shakespeare should unite
Nature's Disjunctions. But the ill-humoured Critic will ask, how
absurd is this? Answer, Can it be absurd that the Poet should be so
unnatural as to put Nature right? But was there ever so pathetic a
Stroke of the Lyre, as the Personification of *Child* for *Childhood*?
This is absolutely brushing Poetry with 'The Whirlwind's Wing',
without attending to the English Language.[1]

He indicates that he may continue his discussion of the
Ode in a later letter and after one of Garrick's friends
has written a letter (September the 19th) to defend Garrick's use of certain expressions, Anti-Gnatho replies on
September the 22nd that

. . . a Desire of doing real Justice to poetic Merit has hitherto been
the Object of his Writing. . . .

[1] *The Public Advertiser*, Sept. 16, 1769, 2, col. 4.

NB. Anti-Gnatho is a great Admirer of Theatric Entertainment, and the Freedom of the House conveyed to him in a Box carved out of the genuine Mulberry . . . would have a happy Effect on his Criticism. It would be perhaps more political to bestow this Mark of Respect on the Critic than on that eloquent Historian, inspired Bard and Jubilee Musquetteer, Mr. James Boswell. . . .[1]

From now on and well into October he levelled his attacks at Boswell rather than Garrick.

On October the 13th *Lloyd's Evening Post* carried the announcement of the following publication:

The Ode on Dedicating a Building and erecting a Statue to Le Stue, *Cook to the Duke of Newcastle at Clermont*; with Notes by Martinus Scriblerus, to which are prefixed Testimonies to the Genius and Merits of Le Stue. 4[to]. Nlcol.[2]

The ode, reprinted in part, is a parody and burlesque on Garrick's Dedication Ode. It received brief, indifferent notices in the October issues of the magazines.

After his return to London on Monday, September the 11th, Garrick was kept busy with preparations for the opening of the Drury Lane season on Saturday the 16th. Following the great success of the Ode at Stratford, Garrick planned to stage it as an after-piece at Drury Lane. On September the 30th he gave his first performance of it there to great applause, and it was repeated seven times during the season of 1769–70. However, the performance of it so taxed Garrick's strength that he never acted in the main piece on the same evening. For instance, when on October the 6th *The Beaux' Stratagem* preceded the Ode, Garrick's favourite part of Archer

---

[1] *The Public Advertiser*, Sept. 22, 1769, 2, 3.
[2] *Lloyd's Evening Post*, Oct. 11–13, 1769, 25, 358, 2–3.

was taken over by Thomas King.[1] The King and Queen attended the performance given on October the 12th.

An enthusiastic review of the first performance of the Ode at Drury Lane shows that Garrick had tried to follow, as closely as possible, the arrangements made for the Stratford presentation. See below and p. 70.

Garrick reciting the Ode at Drury Lane
(British Museum)

On the stage was constructed a semicircular building, elegantly festooned and illuminated, with pillars of the Corinthian order; there were benches laid across the middle of this building, which progressively lessened, till they terminated in a point; on these were placed a select band of musicians, under the direction of Dr. Arne, which consisted of above fifty performers. In the middle was placed a fine statue of Shakespeare, above nine feet high, which

[1] Dougald Macmillan ed., *Drury Lane Calendar* 1747–1776, Oxford 1938, 327.

Garrick brought from Ham (his country-house) on this occasion, whilst he sat to the front accompanied on his right by Mrs. Baddeley and Mr. Vernon; and on his left by Mrs. Scott, Miss Radley and Mr. Champness.

Under this disposition the curtain rose, the whole band playing the overture, which with the brilliancy of a very genteel, and crowded audience, gave the most pleasing impressions.

As for comments on the Ode, the writer quotes the passage on the Passions, which by others had been so severely ridiculed, and speaks of the strong effect it had upon the audience:

. . . he attacks the passions in a most masterly manner . . . Of this I have only to say, that the breast that could be unsusceptible during his repetition of it must have parallel feelings with those of the unnatural *Goneril* and *Regan*.

He notices the thunderous applause following the humorous description of Falstaff and remarks:

Falstaff is no doubt a very laughable character from many peculiar circumstances, such as figure, dress, and the many droll difficulties in which he is engaged; but to support this character, precluded from all these advantages, is a task peculiar to Mr. Garrick; and yet so powerfully, and so humourously did he at once enter into this part, that I will appeal to the best theatrical judges who were present, if they ever before received so strong an impression of the character.

After complimenting Dr Arne, the musicians, and singers he ends with high praise for Garrick:

. . . the last chorus terminated a performance that adds another testimony, amongst many others, of the great excellencies of Mr. Garrick, as an actor, and a writer. . . .

I am Yours,

SENTIMENTAL.[1]

[1] *The London Evening Post*, Oct. 3, 1769.

The September issues of the monthly magazines, published at the beginning of October, carried long accounts of the Jubilee, some of which have already been quoted; a few of them used illustrations, thus an excellent copperplate showing 'Garrick reciting the Ode at Stratford' (see illustration p. 70) appeared in *The Town and Country Magazine*[1] and a full-page plate of 'Boswell in the dress of a Corsican Chief' was published in *The London Magazine* (see p. 97 and illustration p. 99). It is rather surprising in the September and October issues of *The Oxford Magazine* to find two full-page copperplates with these titles: *The Procession at the Jubilee at Stratford upon Avon* (September, p. 103) and *Continuation of the Procession of Shakespeare's Characters* (October, p. 136). A small footnote at the end of the September issue (p. 108) offers this explanation:

The procession of Shakespeare's characters, which was intended at Stratford-upon-Avon and was obliged to be declined on account of the wetness of the weather, was to have been as represented on the copperplate annexed.

The October issue prints the following letter (p. 136):

To the Editors of the Oxford Magazine.
Gentlemen,
I have sent you the continuation of Shakespeare's Characters; and I hope you will cause them to be engraved for the entertainment of your readers. – See page 103.

I am, Sir, your most humble servant,

S. P.

Thus at least the first of these plates must have been prepared before the Jubilee, and although no procession was held there, the editors liked the plates so well that

[1] *The Town and Country Magazine*, Sept. 1769, i, facing p. 472.

they published them anyhow. See illustration, facing
p. 119. To help the reader in identifying the characters
they have captions issuing from their mouths in the form
of a quotation from the play to which they belong. A few
of these captions are so blurred that they cannot be
deciphered.

During September and October, while the Jubilee was
still a topic of general interest to the public, many
writers exploited the fact by making highly varied use
of it in poems, plays, dramatic dialogues, etc., and some
of these writings soon appeared in print. A few of these
will be discussed, as it is possible to gain a little more
knowledge about the Jubilee from them once due allowance is made for humorous, satirical, and malicious
exaggerations.

George Saville Carey's *Shakespeare's Jubilee, A Masque*,
which pays genuine homage to Shakespeare, Garrick,
and the Jubilee, must, however, be placed in a category
by itself, as it was written and published before the
Jubilee and was for sale there.[1]

This masque is composed of two very distinct parts.
The early part is written in rather heavy and often
awkward heroic couplets interspersed with short light
lyrics. These songs are written to popular tunes often
borrowed from the pantomimes and carefully indicated
in the book. The theme of the masque is highly appropriate. The slight action takes place in the last hours of
the night and the early morning before the opening of
the Jubilee. Hecate summons the witches telling them to
fly to Stratford, and unseen to participate in the festival.

---

[1] George Saville Carey, *Shakespeare's Jubilee, A Masque*. London: Printed
for T. Becket and P. A. De Hondt in the Strand. 1769. Carey is known as a
minor writer of songs, satires, an interlude, and a comedy.

After they have left, Oberon appears ordering the fairies to go to Stratford for the same purpose. [Dibdin and Bickerstaffe also used the summoning of the fairies to participate in the Jubilee in their cantata 'Queen Mab' which was performed in Stratford.] Puck now joins them and entertains them with an amusing account of how a puritan and a tailor started fighting in a London tavern when the Jubilee was mentioned and nobody really knew what it was. This satirical verse narrative is written with great spirit. Just as the fairies are ready to leave, they discover Falstaff approaching them, staggering along the road, wondering why he has been summoned from his mouldering tomb and whether he is a ghost or alive. Invisible but audible to him, Puck and the fairies tease him with their voices and urge him to go with them to the Jubilee, where there will be plenty of sack, which tempts him. Suddenly they depart, leaving him alone to sing a song in praise of sack. The witches then re-appear in thunder and lightning, frightening him badly, especially when one orders him to mount on her broomstick and fly to Stratford with them. Afraid, he refuses to go, but they force him to mount and then fly away with him. With this episode the first part comes to an end.

In contrast to this part, where humorous incidents are provided by Puck and Falstaff, the second part is strictly ceremonial and ritualistic. Shakespeare's genius, speaking in solemn blank verse, summons Night, Aurora, Flora, and finally Apollo to appear. The splendid procession that follows would tax the ingenuity of producers and technicians, however familiar with the special demands of the court masque. The author gives the following detailed directions:

GRAND MARCH IS PLAYED

NIGHT ascends with a starry mantle, drawn with dragons through the air. Aurora with a taper, representing twilight; with garlands of flowers, which blossom in her hands. As she walks gently down the stage, birds are heard to sing, and soft music as in the air; the rays of the sun appear in the greatest glory, and the clouds seem all fretted with gold; the light increases, and discovers a magnificent and extensive temple, with cherubim playing, sitting on festoons and wreaths of flowers, which are twined about most beautiful columns of sapphire and gold. Apollo rises as the Sun. Flora, with a basket of flowers, and a garland on her head, scattering flowers as she walks along the temple. Ceres, decorated with her implements of harvest, and a wreath of corn; Pomona, with a cornucopia; Minerva in a chariot of polished steel, drawn by lions; Diana, with her quiver; Tragedy and Comedy in their proper habits, followed by the nine Muses, the fairy King and Queen and a band of Fairies. Witches descend in thunder, and introduce Falstaff. Caliban, Pistol, and all SHAKESPEARE'S favourite Characters, walk two and two down the temple, Apollo comes forward, his chair rises, when appears a pair of lofty gates, he opens them and discovers the statue of SHAKESPEARE. (pp. 20–21.)

Whereupon Apollo, assisted by the chorus, sings his Ode, in which he asks the Muses, the dryads, the naiads, the sylphs, the gnomes, and

> Such sprites as owe
> To his creative boundless muse,
>   Their existence, birth, and name,
>   Come and revel to his fame;
> What mortal, sprite, or fairy can deny,
> To sing their master's immortality.

The final lines sung by the chorus lead to the crowning of the statue:

Sound, sound, the trump, the trump of fame
Proclaim immortal SHAKESPEARE's name;
Fav'rite of Nature and the Nine
Around his head the laurel twine.

FINIS. (pp. 22–23.)

A masque is seldom satisfactory when read, and the reviewers dismissed it with a few brief lines. It is reasonable to suppose that the author had hoped to see it staged at a nobleman's house or country seat about the time of the Jubilee, but no record of any such performance has been found. If it had been given a full production, with adequate music and singing and the magnificent spectacle of the procession and the crowning of the statue, at a time when enthusiasm for Shakespeare ran high, the spectators might well have forgotten or forgiven the poet's occasional lack of skill in handling metre and imagery. It is a good indication of the wide interest Garrick had managed to arouse in the coming Jubilee that such an elaborate masque, aiming to appeal to the taste of the fashionable visitors expected at Stratford, should have been composed well in advance of the event.

The humorous and satirical uses of the Jubilee by authors who had attended it are of a very different order. Captain Edward Thompson's lengthy poem *Trinculo's Trip to the Jubilee* is an early example of this.[1] He must have sent the first part of it to the printers in London, while he himself remained in Stratford, for on September the 7th, the second day of the Jubilee, the following notice appeared in *The St James Chronicle*:

---

[1] Capt. Edward Thompson, *Trinculo's Trip to the Jubilee*. The Second Edition. London: Printed for C. Moran . . . etc. 1769.

In the press and speedily will be published Trinculo's Trip to the Jubilee. Printed for the author and sold by C. Moran at Shakespeare's Head, Tavistock Road, Covent Garden; . . .[1]

When it was published in November 1769 it became so popular that a second edition was issued before the end of the year. It received brief notices in the November issues of the magazines. This poem of forty-seven pages is a very strange medley. One critic wrote:

> There is much of what may be termed *poetic gamboling* and *revelry* in this wild, whimsical droll, *disorderly* poem. It is written in the character of a jolly and humourous tar;
>
> Our greatest objection* to this piece is *its length*. Had the Author, or some judicious friend, corrected and reduced it to half its present quantity, he might have kept his readers in a hearty laugh from the beginning to the end of his motley and merry performance.
>
> * A few indelicacies (too frequent in all the writings of this Gentleman) might also be objected to; but the Author, perhaps, in the present instance, thought them more specially allowable in a production which seems confined to no rules and limitations.[2]

With regard to versification the author certainly follows no rules. He varies his metre, the length of his lines, and his rhyme scheme and makes frequent use of repetitions and refrains. All this makes it possible for him to change the pace of his poem to suit his highly varied material and contributes to its humorous and rollicking effect. The poem opens with his departure from Kew and gives a vivid picture of the heavy traffic on the road to Stratford:

[1] *The St James Chronicle*, Sept. 7–10, 1769, 3, col. 2.
[2] *The Monthly Review*, Nov. 1769, 41, 393–4.

K

> Where chaises came in upon coaches,
> And coaches came in upon chaise;
> The streets, and the inns, and the very highways,
> Were nothing but chaises and coaches,
> And nothing but coaches and chaise. (p. 8.)

Upon their arrival in Stratford they passed 'the booth, sweet Pleasures pride' and drove to the White Lion Inn.

> Yards and streets were full of char'ots,
> Women squalling out like parrots:
> Some were hunting for a bed,
> Some upon the stairs were spread:
> Doodle, doodle, doo.

He then skips to the breakfast in the Town Hall the next morning, where he witnesses a quarrel between Foote and Victor, and comments briefly on the oratorio in the church:

> Where music divine,
> Inspir'd by the NINE
> Inchants the wond'ring earth, and floats along the air.
> (p. 13.)

He devotes two satirical stanzas to the blasphemous Foote in the church. He next describes with broad humour the struggle to get into the amphitheatre for dinner; the long wait for the food, and the free-for-all when it finally arrived; the further confusion when the music began and people wanted to change their seats and in their hurry upset tables and benches and finally the ballad singing:

> Now the catch, and now the glee,
> To the Bard — and Mulb'ry tree:
> But let it be carrol'd, and let it be said,
> That the worst of all beds is a *Warwickshire* bed. (pp. 18–19.)

This did not prevent the author from sleeping soundly after he came back from the hall at four a.m. until, to his annoyance, he was awakened by the serenaders:

> Oh! curse such mattin serenade,
> Cat-cut[1] run mad in high parade,
>   Is likest to the night-mare. (p. 21.)

After breakfast at the Town Hall he went to the amphitheatre to hear the Ode:

> . . . . .
>
> The Ode had all the merit;
> GARRICK superior stood alone,
> His usual brightness he outshone;
>   Out-top'd his former spirit.
>
> Immortal GARRICK be thy name,
> Entwin'd with thy own SHAKESPEARE's fame! (p. 22.)

He continues his praise of the Ode for four stanzas and ends:

> Enraptur'd all retir'd again,
> Full of the high melodious strain,
>   Which Garrick spoke and wrote;
> The Ode it was so *hellish* good,
> We did not mind or rain, or mud,
> Or coach, or chair, or coat.

His comments on some of the characters at the masquerade are amusing:

> Vain Boswell here stood like a Corsican drest,
> Distributing[2] lines which he writ

[1] *cat-cut*; this is no printer's error for catgut. Thompson uses this form (which is not mentioned in *O.E.D.*) several times.

[2] This is an error, Boswell did not get his ode from the printer in time to distribute it, see p. 95.

'Twould have puzzled e'en Shakespeare, to say which were best,
His poesy, hist'ry, or wit. (p. 29.)

. . . . . .

Master Slender was there, but not slender in limb,
He was wondrous thick 'bout the head;
His humour and wit were as slender as him,
And *mum* was the best that he said. (p. 31.)

Finally, he introduces himself with 'a nautical song':

2. I suppose you don't know me, because you all stare,
   You see I'm a sailor, as such I can swear,
   But remember 'Tis TRINCULO, so have a care.
   Of his up and down, up and down, high derry
   up and down, high derry down.

3. With Shakespeare I sail'd in a *Tempest* of yore,
   We had land's-men on board of the quality *corps*,
   And were shipwrecked by Jove on a comical shore.
   With his up and down, etc.

. . . . . .

9. Let this toast then be drank from old Dublin to Warwick,
   Resounded again from dull Dover to Berwick,
   To sweet Willy Shakespeare and gay Davy Garrick.
   With their up and down, etc.

(pp. 32–34.)

He mentions that he waded in dirt to the knees when he left the masquerade to go to his lodgings. The last part of the poem is not based on any actual happenings at the Jubilee. The author gives his imagination free rein in inventing a contest for a cup in which writers compete to see who can dive deepest into the mud of the Avon; it is obviously an imitation of a similar contest in Book II of Pope's *Dunciad*. It gives him an opportunity for witty and sharp remarks about the participants, among whom he includes writers that did not attend the Jubilee, such as Johnson and Goldsmith. The poem drones on to a very weak and ineffective ending.

But in spite of some boring passages in this long-winded, chaotic, and 'disorderly' poem the author manages at times to catch the Jubilee mood of boisterous gaiety and merriment.

On September the 18th *The London Chronicle* mentions the publication of an anonymous pamphlet: 'Garrick's *Vagary*: *or* England *run Mad*; *with Particulars* of the Stratford Jubilee.'[1] This is a prose medley in six scenes of dramatic dialogue in which some direct exposition by the author and some indifferent verses are included. The prologue and the epilogue are in rhymed verse. Here is a more ambitious, but certainly much less successful, attempt than Thompson's to criticize the Jubilee. One magazine calls it 'A performance attempted in the manner of a dramatic tale, without the least shadow of poetical merit'.[2] Another scornfully says, 'We dare affirm that this delightful vagary will be read by few besides the unfortunate reviewers'.[3] It does, however, throw light on certain aspects of the Jubilee.

In the 'Preface' the author gives a lengthy explanation of his reasons for choosing the peculiar form he has given the pamphlet. After this comes 'The Prologue':

O for the Genius of laughing Dean *Swift*,
For who could a Joke set better adrift?
Grant me, kind *Momus*, with Humour to tell,
What Scenes at *Stratford on Avon* befell:
O vary my Style as the Subject flows,
Now ambling in Rhime, now trotting in Prose. . . . (p. viii.)

---

[1] *The London Chronicle*, Sept. 17–19, 1769, **26**, 277, 1.
[2] *The Gentleman's Magazine*, Sept. 1769, **39**, 454.
[3] *The London Magazine*, Oct. 1769, **38**, 537.

The rather ambitious purpose of the pamphlet is clearly stated in the concluding paragraph of the last scene:

Under the Masks of several fancied Characters, I have attempted to convey the different Opinions of different Minds as well as my own, for and against the late Jubilee, and incidental Events, without, it is hoped, any Body's taking Offence thereat, because none was meant. . . . (p. 54.)

To show the different attitudes taken towards the Jubilee the author takes us to The Bedford Coffee-House and presents 'three critical Play-house Frequenters', Nettle, an irascible, choleric man; Lurcher, who likes to make sarcastic remarks; and Fanciful, a light-hearted, fashionable wag. Nettle is angry and full of complaint, and he voices great indignation against the people of England for:

. . . running out of Town, pell-mell, after a Brat of *Judaism*, a since foster-child of *Popery*, now, forsooth, revived by an Actor, to the very imminent and most alarming Danger both of Church and State. . . . (pp. 3–4.)

When the others try to interrupt him with smart remarks he insists on proceeding with an incredibly long-winded exposition of the word Jubilee, its origin and 'Intendment' so that:

. . . we may be enabled justly to ascertain with what Propriety this Term is now forced, or rather perverted, to notify and misdecorate a new Species of Bacchanalian Revelling at Stratford upon Avon. (p. 7.)

This scene serves to draw attention to some of the absurd and vicious talk about popery in connexion with the Jubilee, but it is far too long and boring. It covers fourteen pages.

Next Nettle asks, 'What necessity was there for an Oratorio?' Fanciful has a ready answer, 'Because, I suppose, no other kind of Performance would be allowed of in the Church.' When Lurcher asks, 'Why was a choice made of *Judith*?' Fanciful says:

Why the reason is very obvious – there being no Oratorio called *William* to be done in immediate honour of himself, a judicious Approximation was thus made, he having had no Sons, by complimenting him thro' his eldest Daughter *Judith* – [1] (pp. 21–22.)

The others get so annoyed with his flippant remarks that they leave in disgust.

Scene II is laid at an inn on the road to Stratford where Hemlock and Crotchet, two disgruntled and envious authors whose plays Garrick had refused to produce, are plotting how best to disturb the Jubilee proceedings, thereby bringing ridicule and disgrace to Garrick and his collaborators. All their sinister plotting comes to nothing. This recalls Foote's threats about disrupting the ceremonies at Stratford. This scene is also much too long to hold the reader's interest.

So far the pamphlet has reflected the spiteful views of Garrick's enemies. In the next three scenes, all set in Stratford during the Jubilee, the author presents the attitude taken by some of the actor's friends and admirers. Only two characters, and they remain the same throughout, Sir Benjamin Scrutiny and Lord Charles Candid, discuss their experiences in these scenes. The bitter, tense atmosphere of the first two scenes has now disappeared; everything is pleasant and cheerful. The

---

[1] Judith was Shakespeare's younger daughter, the elder was named Susannah.

men are pleased with their lodgings, from which they can watch the gay crowds in the street below; so much so that Lord Charles gets excited about all this activity and starts writing poetry about it 'in what the People of Fashion are pleased to call the easy Gentleman-like Stile'. They leave to attend the Oratorio.

When we next encounter them a day has passed; they are walking in the street on their way to the Booth to hear the Ode. Sir Benjamin has just got rid of an extremely ill-natured and fault-finding man who is envious of Garrick for having planned the Jubilee and become its Steward. Sir Benjamin had answered that 'no other Individual could have been the principal Agent here, with so much Propriety'. By producing and acting in Shakespeare's plays Garrick had won fame and 'an ample Fortune; a Part whereof cannot, surely, be better employed than on an Occasion like this'. Sir Charles is 'not only pleased with but obliged to Mr. Garrick, for his having been chiefly instrumental in so commendable, nay so patriotic an Institution'. They both agree that if the purpose is worthy, a generous mind should make allowance for unforeseen accidents, such as the rain that spoiled the procession and the fire-works (pp. 38–39). They see the good-looking Mr Angelo go by 'with folded Arms and down-cast Eyes muttering to himself with discontented Accents – now in Italian . . . now in French . . . what bad Weather!' Sir Benjamin feels sorry for him, for 'he has taken uncommon Pains to make a most elegant Apparatus of Fireworks' (p. 40). Then they go on towards the Booth to hear the Ode.

Scene V takes place the following morning, the day of their departure. Lord Charles went to the masquerade the night before and found it brilliant; Sir Benjamin,

strongly disapproving of masquerades, stayed at home
and was visited by an odd, whimsical student from the
Temple who discussed the ridiculous behaviour of some
of the authors attending the Jubilee, and their arrogant,
contemptuous attitude towards their fellow authors.
This refers to criticism of Garrick's Ode (pp. 49–51).

The last scene is set in '*the* Apollo *Room at the* Shakespeare's *Head*, Covent Garden' where the members of
the Mulberry Club are holding their weekly meeting,
'*sitting round a Table, on which is a Representation of the*
Mulberry *Tree*'. The author has just finished report-
ing on his trip to Stratford, whereupon they sing *The
Epilogue*:

. . . . . .

> *Life's* but a *Catch*; who can laugh is the *Man*:
> Come fill up your Glasses, honour my Toast,
> The *Laurel* to him who prais'd Shakespeare most.
> Envy defeated is in a Quandary,
> While we Bumpers drink to *Garrick's Vagary*;
> Can Homage so just make *England run mad*?
> No; false is the Charge: all Worthies 'twill glad,
>   Let Critics dissent, or let them agree,
> We'll sing, and dance round the Mulberry-tree. (p. 55.)

Thus after having sketched the opinions of some of
Garrick's enemies and friends with regard to the Jubilee,
the author in the Epilogue pays homage to Garrick and
his 'vagary' and admits that the title of the pamphlet is
perhaps somewhat misleading. He should be given re-
cognition for a highly original approach to his topic.

On September the 19th, the day after *Garrick's
Vagary* had appeared, *The London Chronicle* printed the
following notice:

This Day was published, Price 1 sh. sewed.

THE STRATFORD JUBILEE

A new Comedy of Two Acts, as it has lately been exhibited at Stratford upon Avon with great Applause. To which is added *Scrub's Trip to the Jubilee*, a comic Prologue spokent his Night at the Theatre Royal in the Haymarket, by Mr. Weston.

Printed for T. Lowndes, No: 77, Fleet Street;
and J. Bell, near Exeter Change, in the Strand.¹

No Author's name was given, but it was an open secret that it was the work of Francis Gentleman, known in the theatrical world for his comedies and his altered versions of Ben Jonson's *Alchemist* and *Sejanus*. As for the statement on the title page that it 'has lately been exhibited at Stratford upon Avon with great Applause', no record of this seems to exist, but it may possibly refer to performances (or readings?) before a private audience. The play is dedicated to Samuel Foote. In an address 'To the Public', Gentleman offers the following explanation:

The author thinks it incumbent upon him to observe, that the following Occasional Piece was imagined, and put into its present State within the Space of a very few Days and has some Reason to believe, that it would have been presented at the Theatre Royal in the Haymarket, if the Thought had been suggested in Time for Mr. FOOTE's Season. Some kind, and perhaps partial Friends, urged the Publication, it thus steps into Life with *many Imperfections on its Head;* . . .

Foote was wise in declining the comedy, for it is quite weak. As all the slight, trivial action takes place in Stratford on the day before the Jubilee without any reference to later events, Gentleman may well have started writing it during the festival itself. He uses type

¹ *The London Chronicle*, Sept. 17–19, 1769, **26**, 278, 3.

names for most of his characters, such as Lord Spangle, Sir John Hearty, Sir Charles Planwell, Scrape-all, a stingy, wealthy London businessman, Longcork, the waiter, Lady Shanker, a fanatic horse breeder and race-goer, and Captain Blarney, a bragging Irishman. They all live up to their names and are slightly caricatured. At one time or another all of them go to the warehouse to rent costumes for the masquerade at exorbitant prices. There are a few humorous incidents where glib sales talk makes the customers choose highly inappropriate costumes.

In this play we have an excellent example of the use of the day before the Jubilee as a setting for a rather dull little domestic comedy. It does convey the feeling of the crowds and the fact that all sorts of people were gathered there, but while the warehouse scene is mildly entertaining, the play as a whole is weak and shows signs of being hastily put together.

There is nothing very remarkable about *Scrub's Trip to the Jubilee*, the poem prefixed to Gentleman's play as a sort of Prologue. Scrub, the clownish country servant in Farquhar's *The Beaux' Stratagem*, was a favourite comic character with the audiences at Drury Lane, but the poem he recites is disappointing. It mentions the great crowds, the Ode, the rain, and the poor beds. It is not surprising that Scrub does not care for turtle, but would prefer beef neck. A brief quotation will suffice:

> I drank too — and now I a poet may be —
> From a charming fine cup of the mulberry tree.
> To bed I must go — for which like a ninny
> I paid — like my betters — no less than a guinea.
> For rolling — not sleeping — in linen so damp
> As struck my great toe ever since with the cramp. . . .
>
> (ll. 31–36.)

All the pieces just discussed have very little, if any, literary value and probably had a very limited circulation; the authors obviously wanted to exploit an event very widely discussed in order to present their own impressions and opinions of it. But in so doing they bear vivid testimony to the continued general interest shown in the festival weeks after it was over, an interest that was not limited to Garrick's friends and foes.

IV

The Jubilee on the London Stage: The Rival Managers

None of the pieces discussed in the last chapter attempted to give stage versions of the more official but cancelled features of the Jubilee such as the procession or pageant. It is true, Carey ended his masque with a final crowning of Shakespeare's statue, also cancelled at Stratford; but this was not so much a stage version of what should have taken place, as a fitting highly spectacular ending to his own piece.

Now Colman and Garrick enter upon the scene both busy with Jubilee pieces. Colman was engaged in the adaptation of a domestic comedy to a Stratford setting, so that he could insert the Pageant and, in dumbshow, the masquerade into his production at Covent Garden; whereas Garrick for his at Drury Lane put the main emphasis on the splendid staging of the Pageant and the final scene with the crowning of Shakespeare's statue. He supplied a very slight framework for this.

London was much amused by the rivalry between the two managers. The story of their efforts will now be told.

The September issue of *The Town and Country Magazine* gives some news about the Royal Theatres:

The theatre-royal in Haymarket closed for the season on Friday September 15, and the next day Drury-lane theatre opened with

The Clandestine Marriage [by Colman and Garrick] and High Life below Stairs. On the Monday following Covent Garden theatre was opened with the opera of Love in a Village, and the Miller of Mansfield.

Nothing new hath yet appeared at either house, but we are in expectation of several new pieces, as well as fresh performers. Among the former is a *petite* piece of three acts, by Mr. Colman, entitled, Man and Wife; or, the Stratford Jubilee.[1]

Garrick, who was busily engaged in the staging of his own Jubilee piece at Drury Lane, must have known about Colman's efforts, for in a letter to Joseph Cradock, dated October the 2nd, in which he thanks him for his assistance at Stratford, he writes, 'We are preparing to Jubilee it upon the stage. Mr. Colman enters the lists with us much to my surprise.'[2] Colman managed to write and stage his three-act comedy *Man and Wife; or The Shakespeare Jubilee* in time for a first performance at Covent Garden on October the 7th when it was announced in *The Public Advertiser*:

COVENT GARDEN

NEVER PERFORMED.

At the Theatre Royal Covent Garden, This day
will be presented

A new comedy of Three Acts called

MAN and WIFE:
Or, The SHAKESPEARE JUBILEE

. . . .

[A list of the actors follows but not of the characters in the play.]

[1] *The Town and Country Magazine*, I, 456.
[2] Cradock, op. cit., I, 219.

With a PRELUDE,

End of Act II, a PAGEANT

Exhibiting the CHARACTERS of SHAKESPEARE.

End of Act III.

A Representation of the AMPHITHEATRE at

STRATFORD upon AVON,

With a MASQUERADE.

To which will be added a Ballad Opera called

DAMON AND PHILLIDA, . . .[1]

. . . .

The comedy was published in November 1769[2] but dated 1770,[3] with a dedication to Sir Joshua Reynolds, a fellow member of Dr Johnson's Literary Club, of which Colman had been elected a member on February 18th, 1768. In a review of the play in *The St James Chronicle*, dated October the 10th, the following statement occurs:

The Stratford Jubilee having been designed and conducted by Mr. Garrick, it was natural to expect, that the Exhibition upon the Banks of the Avon, would prove a Kind of Rehearsal of a Spectacle to be represented during the Winter at Drury-Lane Theatre, and that the Pageant and Masquerade, together with the Transparencies, Illuminations, etc., would compose a capital Part of some new Entertainment, in conducting which, the Steward of the Jubilee would return to his old Province of Manager; but we must fairly confess, that we did not expect to find so early a Use made of that Celebrity on the Stage of Covent Garden. Necessity they say is the Mother of Invention, and perhaps the heavy Loss sustained by this Author, in the Death of the late Mr. Powell,

[1] *The Public Advertiser*, Oct. 7, 1769, 1, col. 1.
[2] *The Gentleman's Magazine*, Nov. 1769, 39, 549.
[3] Colman, George (the Elder), *Man and Wife | or, the | Shakespeare Jubilee | A | Comedy, | of three Acts, | As it is Performed at the | Theatre Royal in Covent Garden, London, Printed for T. Becket. . . . 1770.

induced him to turn his Thoughts forward to this Undertaking, in which we think he acquitted himself very happily, though very hastily.[1]

In mentioning this play, the theatre historian, Mr Benjamin Victor, had this to say:

MAN and WIFE or, the *Shakespeare Jubilee*, a Comedy of two Acts, by George Colman, Esq.

The Jubilee at *Stratford upon Avon* in Honour of *Shakespeare*, which was celebrated there at the Entrance of the preceding Month, was invented and conducted by Mr. *Garrick*, at great Expence and Trouble, furnished the Hint for this Piece, which Mr. *Colman* availed himself of, by bringing it on Covent Garden Theatre, before that Exhibition at *Drury-Lane* could be got ready.

Though this Transaction has been differently spoken of, yet it must be confessed to have been the Practice, Time immemorial, of the Managers of contending Theatres. This Entertainment was performed several Nights and well received by the Public.[2]

Colman seems nevertheless to have suffered from a slightly bad conscience on account of his having presented his play with the Procession and the Masquerade a week ahead of Garrick's Jubilee piece, in an attempt to steal some of his thunder. This is revealed indirectly in the interesting 'Prelude' to his comedy which opens with a dialogue between two men who are looking at the new playbill outside the Covent Garden Theatre. They are joined by little Dapperwit, the manager [Colman's apt name for himself] who is in mourning for a dear actor-friend who has died recently and to whom he pays sincere homage. This refers to the well-known actor William Powell, who had died late in July. Then the

[1] *The St James Chronicle*, Oct. 7–10, 1769, 4, col. 2.
[2] Victor, op. cit., 3, 163–4.

two men tease him about aiming 'a stroke at the Jubilee' in his new comedy. He answers:

An innocent laugh, Sir, raised out of an adventure, which, I have taken the liberty to suppose, happened during that period. As to the Jubilee itself, or the design or conduct of it, I cannot consider them as objects of satire. (p. III.)

The others quote a few lines from Foote's definition to show that the Jubilee has been subject to attack and satirical treatment, whereupon Dapperwit defends Foote under the name of Pasquin:

. . . his pleasantries are exceedingly harmless, and I believe he wishes they should be so. — The scandal of others is mere dirt — throw a great deal, and some of it will stick. But the satire of Pasquin is like fuller's earth — it daubs your coat indeed for a time, but it soon grows dry; and when it rubs off, your coat is so much the cleaner. — Thus it happened on the present occasion — for, after all, gentlemen, if a building be erected for a particular purpose, is not it natural to pull it down again, when that purpose is answered? A great number of people cannot be assembled without creating a croud — a rainy day will prevent the exhibition of a pageant — and heavy showers destroy the effect of a firework. (pp. III–IV.)

When the 'ode without poetry' is mentioned, Dapperwit points out that 'it had one capital fault, . . . I understood every word of it. Now, an ode, they say, — an ode — to be very good, should be wholly unintelligible' (p. IV). He informs them that the Ode is not incorporated into his play and enters upon the most high-flown, almost fulsome praise of Garrick and the Ode:

No — the ode can no where be heard to so much advantage as from the mouth of the author — and indeed it was so happily calculated for the time and place, for which it was originally intended,

L

and the speaker so truly felt a noble enthusiasm on the occasion, that you have lost a very exquisite pleasure (never to be retrieved) by not hearing it at Stratford-upon-Avon. (p. IV.)

He ends by saying that they will see the pageant and the masquerade in the play, whereupon they enter the theatre. The whole situation is aptly discussed in a review of the play that appeared in *The Town and Country Magazine*:

The prelude, as it is called, is an humble imitation of Mr. Foote's introductory dialogue to the Minor. The Manager, conscious that he lived last year upon Mr. Garrick's Masquerade, and that he was in the present case purloining his pageant procession, offers incense to the Drury-Lane Chief, till every nostril is offended. It was pleasantly said by Mr. Foote that it put him in mind of a *Ludgate-hill Prostitute* tickling Mr. G — with one hand, and picking his pocket with the other.[1]

Like Francis Gentleman, Colman uses the Jubilee as a setting for a domestic comedy, and though just as hastily written, his is a much better play. The somewhat complicated plot is the old, well-tried farcical one of a wealthy citizen of London and his quarrelsome wife, here Mr and Mrs Cross, unable to agree on anything and certainly not on which of her two suitors their daughter Charlotte should marry. The father favours Mr Kitchen (aptly named, for his only hobby and topic of conversation is food), a wealthy, respectable, straightforward, but rather dull London citizen. The mother's choice offers a sharp contrast, for she prefers Marcourt, an empty-headed spendthrift and haughty fashionable coxcomb, with affected speech and manners, strongly reminiscent of the arrogant Macaroni played by Thomas

[1] *The Town and Country Magazine*, Oct. 1769, I, 547, I.

King after the recitation of the Ode at Stratford. Charlotte, however, has fallen in love with honest Colonel Freeman[1] but has kept this a secret from her parents. This situation lends itself to endless intrigues and much deception on the part of Charlotte before the happy union of the lovers is finally achieved. The plot has several points of similarity with the story of Ann Page and her three suitors in Shakespeare's *The Merry Wives of Windsor*. It could be placed against almost any background, provided that there is some sort of masquerade at the end offering an opportunity for the use of mistaken identity for the solution of the plot.

It is interesting to observe how Colman makes use of the Jubilee as a setting for his plot. Act I is quite good. It is set in the hall of the Inn very early in the morning of the second day of the festival. Great confusion reigns, with visitors' bells ringing, waiters scurrying around, people drinking and singing snatches of 'The Warwickshire Lad'. Into this chaos the three suitors arrive one by one. When Marcourt is asked whether he has come to walk in the pageant, he replies scornfully that he is not interested in Shakespeare and asks the host what the Jubilee is all about; he knows only of the Jubilee in Rome. Kitchen, his rival, expresses a liking for Shakespeare, which offers an opportunity for Marcourt to voice his contempt for Shakespeare's 'barbarous farces, as uncouth a medley to present to this age as a pageant or a puppet-show. – No foreigners can endure him' (p. 18). This leads to a heated discussion between them.

In Act II Marcourt has convinced Mrs Cross that it is the height of fashion to invite friends to come to one's house in costume for a party before the masquerade. She

---

[1] In the printed version Colman has changed his name to Frankly.

is planning such a party on a large scale for seven o'clock that night. At the end of Act II the pageant of Shakespeare's characters is inserted without any attempt at linking it with the action; none of the characters in the play mention it. Colman was out to beat Garrick at his own game and proud of having staged the procession a week before Garrick's piece was ready. It is highly probable that, belonging to one of the theatres, he had been asked to walk in the cancelled procession at Stratford, thus he must have seen an outline of the order of the pageant with its main divisions, the many plays represented and the characters chosen from them, so that he was able to produce quite a good representation of it on the Covent Garden stage. His main divisions are correct, most of the plays and characters represented come close to those in Garrick's *The Jubilee*; he has the tragic and the comic muses with their retinues and Shakespeare's bust drawn in a chariot. It does not tally in all details with Garrick's pageant in *The Jubilee*. Colman's groups are small, often there are only two characters and even in a few cases just one. No banners are carried with the names of the plays, so that the spectators found it hard to identify some of them; yet it made a favourable impression on the audiences as a spectacular novelty.

Act III follows with Mrs Cross's pre-masquerade party, where Charlotte outwits both her parents, and while her maid appears in her mistress's costume, Charlotte slips away unnoticed to join Colonel Freeman at the church for their wedding. Whereupon they return to the house to ask her parents' forgiveness for her deception, which being granted without too much difficulty, since neither father nor mother have gained their point, the whole party proceeds to the Amphitheatre for the Masquerade. After Act III comes the spectacle of the Amphitheatre with the Masquerade in progress. This is indicated on the play-bill and in the newspaper announcements, but is omitted in the earliest printed version of the play, which has the three-act division. Later Colman omitted both the pageant and the Amphitheatre scenes, and the play was then stated to be in two acts (see p. 146).

The play was eagerly awaited:

Mr Colman's comedy, entitled *Man and Wife*, or *The Shakespeare Jubilee*, was represented for the first time at Covent-Garden theatre, on Saturday the 9th of this month, to a very crowded audience, the house being filled almost as soon as the doors were opened, so eager was the town to pay attention to this offspring of the manager's brain; . . .[1]

It was quite well received; even the review printed on October the 10th in *The St James Chronicle*, of which Garrick was part-owner, commended it:

The Prelude is extremely new and entertaining . . . The Bustle and Business of the first Act is very spirited; the Characters of Mr. and Mrs. Cross, though obvious, are well sustained; and those of Kitchin and Marcourt are an exact Copy of the Coxcomb and *Bon Vivant* of the day. . . . The Pageant and the Masquerade are with much Address annexed to this Comedy, and have a happy Effect; though they are each capable of and perhaps will severally receive many Improvements.[2]

The London Chronicle of October the 5th–8th devotes no less than three long columns to an outline of the action and a somewhat detailed account of the pageant, but offers no comment. In the October issue of *The Town*

---

[1] *The Town and Country Magazine*, Oct. 1769, I, 545, I.
[2] *The St James Chronicle*, Oct. 10, 1769, 4, col. I.

and Country Magazine quoted above there is, besides an outline, an interesting account of the pageant with details of the incidental music by Dr Arnold. Some unkind remarks are made about the comedy and the acting, and the pageant is severely criticized:

The pageant at the end of the second act, is merely introduced to forestal the original inventor. It has no connection with the business of the play; and as it is represented, is an absolute dead march.

Mr. Colman's friends, indeed, acknowledge that it was a hasty production, written in order to gratify the temporary taste of the town.[1]

The London Magazine has a fairly brief review.[2] After the play had appeared in print in November brief critical notices appeared again, some favourable others unfavourable. The play was performed every night of the following week, also on the 14th, when Garrick's afterpiece *The Jubilee* was first performed, to which it was unable to offer proper competition. Brief notices in *The Public Advertiser* tell the story.

October 16 The new comedy of Man and Wife is obliged to be deferred for a few days [for improvements].
October 19 played by command of Their Majesties. . . . MAN AND WIFE.[3]

After this there were a few scattered performances on the same days as Garrick's piece, whereupon Colman retired his play after a total of eleven performances.

On October the 14th, exactly a week after the first performance of Colman's Jubilee play, Garrick could

---

[1] *The Town and Country Magazine*, Oct. 1769, 1, 547, 2.
[2] *The London Magazine*, Oct. 1769, 38, 497, 1.
[3] *The Public Advertiser*, Oct. 16, 1769, 1, col. 1 and Oct. 19, 1769, 1, col. 1.

G. COLMAN Esq.ʳ   *The Rival Managers.*   D. GARRICK Esq.ʳ

The Rival Managers

(from the *Ladies' Magazine*, Sept. 1769)

THE
OVERTURE, SONGS, AIRS, and CHORUSSES,
in the
JUBILEE *or* SHAKESPEAR's GARLAND
as Performed at Stratford *upon* Avon,
and the Theatre Royal Drury Lane.
To which is added a Cantata called
QUEEN MAB or the FAIRIES JUBILEE.
Composed by
CHARLES DIBDIN.

Pr. 6s.

*London Printed & Sold by John Johnston N.º 97 Drury Lane & Longman Lukey & Broderip N.º 26 Cheap
of whom may be had the above adapted for the* Guittar & German Flute.

Title-page to *The Jubilee or Shakespeare's Garland*
(from The Stratford Jubilee, a scrapbook, British Museum)

announce the first performance of his Jubilee piece in
The Public Advertiser:

DRURY-LANE

By his Majesty's Company.
At the Theatre Royal, Drury-Lane this Day will be presented,
THE SCHOOL FOR RAKES . . .

To which will be added (never performed before) an Entertainment
in Two Parts, of Singing, Dancing, and Dialogue, called
THE JUBILEE. . . .

The Vocal Parts by
Mr. Vernon, Mr. Dibdin, Mr. Bannister, Mr. Champness, Mr.
Fawcett, Mr. Kear, etc.
Miss Radley, and Mrs. Baddeley.

The Dances by
Sieur Dagueville, Mrs. King, Signora Vidini,
Miss Rogers, . . .

In which will be introduced

The PAGEANT, as it was intended for STRATFORD upon AVON.
The Music by Mr. Dibdin.
New Scenes, Dresses, and Decorations. . . .[1]

Fairly detailed reviews with outlines of *The Jubilee*
appeared in the newspapers and in the October issues of
the *London Magazine*, *The Town and Country Magazine*,
and others.

The play was not published, but remained in manuscript at Drury Lane. From there it passed into the hands
of John Philip Kemble, the actor-manager, who had a
very large collection of plays (more than nine thousand
items). For nearly a century people believed that the
manuscript had been destroyed in a fire at Drury Lane
Theatre. In 1820 Kemble sold his collection to the

[1] *The Public Advertiser*, Oct. 14, 1769, 1, col. 1.

The principal Characters in the Proce͟ſ͟s
at Drury La

The Proce͟ſs

of the Pageant exhibited in the Jubilee Theatre.

Drury Lane

sixth Duke of Devonshire, who added to it considerably. In January 1914 the Kemble–Devonshire collection was sold to the American collector Mr Henry Edwards Huntington and is now housed in the Huntington Library in California. Professor Elizabeth P. Stein discovered a manuscript of *The Jubilee* in the collection and published it in an annotated edition in 1926 in her book *Three Plays by David Garrick*, pp. 55–113. Professor Stein describes the memoranda on the title page as follows:

On the title page of this play appears a memorandum, written by Garrick of some books he lent to Dr. Burney on Oct. 5, 1771. Following this we find a note by Kemble which reads:

The Jubilee
written by David Garrick, Esq.
The Manuscript Notes, as well as the memoranda at the top of this Page are in Mr. Garrick's Handwriting – J.P.K.
Collated and Perfect J.P.K. 1800.[1]

There can be no doubt about the authenticity of this manuscript. The following account of the piece is based on this, the only printed edition.

Garrick wrote a clever 'Prologue' which was spoken by Thomas King in the character of a London waiter. He tells a story of two ale-houses between Hounslow and Colebroke:

> . . . two *Magpies* by name;
> The one of old standing, the other a new one, –
> That boasts he's the old *one*, and this he's the *true* one. . . .
> A race we have had for your pastime and laughter: –
> *Young Mag* started first, with *old Mag* hopping after:

[1] Elizabeth P. Stein, op. cit., 107–8.

'Tis said the old house had possess'd a receipt,
To make a choice mixture of sour, strong and sweet;
A *Jubilee* punch — with art skilfully made,
Assur'd the *Old Magpie* a good running trade; . . .
Each Magpie, your Honours, will peck at his brother,
And their natures were always to peck at each other;
Young landlords, and *old* ones, are taught by their calling
To hate all engrossing — but practice *forestalling*:
Our *landlords* are *game-cocks* — and fair play but grant 'em
I warrant you pastime from each *little Bantam* —.[1]

These apt metaphors about the two theatres and their managers, who were both short men, caught the fancy of the town and were used by newspaper writers a number of times.

It is interesting to see how Garrick turns events at the Stratford Jubilee into an afterpiece at Drury Lane. He needed a slight framework that would allow him to introduce many of the songs written for the Jubilee and the two important entertainments that had been cancelled on account of the rain, i.e. the procession and the crowning of Shakespeare's statue. The Ode he had already turned into an afterpiece by itself, so that he need not include that. He would want to give some impression of the atmosphere that had prevailed, the bustle, the crowding, even the complaints, to introduce some fairly distinct types such as the old women, the country bumpkins, the Irishman, and the pedlars, and also to show some humorous scenes with noisy crowds. The framework should provide a light, amusing background for the highly spectacular scenes of the procession and the crowning of Shakespeare's statue. He was now able to laugh at his misfortunes at Stratford, to savour some of

---

[1] *The Town and Country Magazine,* Oct. 1769, **1,** 553–4.

the ridiculous happenings, and to make others laugh at
them too. But he was serious about the procession and
the final crowning of the statue and would spare no
costs to make the *Jubilee* at Drury Lane the most impressive spectacle of the whole year. To show how he
achieved this a brief outline of the play is necessary.

The first scene is set very early in the morning in an
old woman's house in Stratford. She is asleep in her chair
when a neighbour wakes her. They gossip and complain
bitterly about the Jubilee and are full of fear and superstition; they are joined by Ralph, a country bumpkin, a
part also played by Thomas King. He is sure that the
Pope is behind the Jubilee, or perhaps the Pretender,
for he has seen men at work with gunpowder in a barn
and at the College and thinks that there is a plot to blow
up the town. He also mentions that he has seen the
Steward, who is a little plump man. When a few minutes
later the cannon are fired for the opening of the Jubilee
they are all frightened and run out.

The stage directions for Scene II read:

> *The Street, with a Post chaise on one side,*
> *Enter Musicians with Singers in Dominos, to give a*
> *Serenade — Ladies look out at a window.*

They sing the air 'Let Beauty with the Sun arise'. An
Irishman, played by Mr Moody, who together with
another man has been sleeping in the post chaise because
he could find no bed, complains at being disturbed by
the singers and asks if this is what you call a Jubilee.
They help him out of the chaise; he is dishevelled and
has to straighten his wig, which he has had to use as a
night-cap; he then listens to the Musician's definition of
a Jubilee. Here Garrick makes clever use of part of

Foote's definition of a Jubilee, putting it in ballad form. It was sung by Mr Bannister, taking off Mr Foote:

> 1. This is Sir a Jubilee
>   Crowded without Company
>   Riot without Jollity
>   That's a Jubilee
>   Thus 'tis night and day Sir
>   I hope that you will stay Sir
>   To see our Jubilee.
>
>   . . . . . .
>
> 3. Odes Sir without Poetry
>   Music without Melody
>   Singing without Harmony.
>   Thus 'tis etc.
>
> 4. Holes to thrust your Head in Sir
>   Lodgings without Bedding Sir
>   Beds as if they'd Lead in Sir
>   Thus 'tis etc.
>
> 5. Blanket without sheeting Sir
>   Dinners without Eating Sir
>   Not without much cheating Sir
>   Thus 'tis etc. (pp. 74–75.)

The Irishman speaks of having been to the Inn 'where all the plays are writ upon the doors, and so I thought to see a play, and pop'd my head into *Much Ado about Nothing* and there was nothing at all but the Steward with his mulberry box upon his breast, speaking his fine Ode to music' (p. 75).

Two ballad singers arrive and sing 'The Warwickshire Lad' . . . Scene III. The White Lyon Inn Yard.

A vivid scene with harassed waiters and hungry people; a man asking for his boots is told that all the

new ones have been taken more than half an hour ago.
Pedlars with souvenirs of mulberry wood appear, accuse
each other of cheating, and are driven away by the
Irishman. Various side-shows are announced by drum
or trumpet. The Irishman finally bribes a waiter to get
him some food and leaves to take a nap while waiting for
the pageant. Then singers, followed by a crowd, arrive
with the Mulberry Cup and sing 'Behold this fair Goblet'; whereupon bells are rung and all leave in a hurry to
see the pageant.

HERE FOLLOWS THE PAGEANT. (pp. 86–92.)

With Bells ringing, fifes play⁹, drums beating, and Canon firing.
Order of the Pageant in the Jubilee.
All enter from the Top of the Stage.

[A note in the MS in Garrick's handwriting reads: 'NB. in the
procession Every Scene in ye different Plays represents some capital
part of it in action.'].[1]

9 Men Dancers with Tambourines / 3 Graces / 9 Women
Dancers – Muses

(They dance down the Stage to Music)

2 Men drest in Old English with Mottos of the Theatre *upon rich*
Standards with proper decorations / 2 fifes / and 2 drums; (p. 86.)

Then follow eight groups from these comedies: *As You
Like It; The Tempest; The Merchant of Venice; Much Ado
About Nothing; Two Gentlemen of Verona; Twelfth Night;
A Midsummer Night's Dream;* and *The Merry Wives of
Windsor.* Each group is led by the bearer of a banner
showing the name of the play in large letters. On an
average four to six characters are included, often preceded or followed by appropriate extras like foresters or
sailors. When the group approaches the proscenium

[1] Elizabeth P. Stein, op. cit., 110.

arch, the main characters mime an important scene in the play as they go by. At this point a note has been inserted in the MS:

Suppose Bottom & Q. of Fs asleep in Ye Chariot – & K. of F. drops her Eyes with the Flower, turns out Bottom, & takes his Place & She awakes &c.[1]

Stage properties carried by the characters are carefully indicated, for instance: 'Rosalind in boys Cloaths with a Crook . . ./Jacques with a Spear, Melancholly/. . . Ariel with a Wand – raising a Tempest/. . . Caliban with a wooden bottle and 2 Sailors all drunk/. . . Two men with the Caskets in a rich [cabinet]/. . . Shylock with a knife, and bond and Scales.' *The Merry Wives of Windsor* has a group of nineteen people, of which some minor characters are drawn from *Henry IV, Part II.* Except for 'Bardolph with a Cup', no stage properties are mentioned for this group, but one wonders about the follow-stage direction: 'Mrs. Ford, Falstaff, Mrs. Page on Horseback'.[2] In the MS a note, not in Garrick's hand, reads:

What is the whim of having these particularly on Horseback? . . . four Fellows sh^d bring In Sr John in Ye Buck Basket Ye Wives on either Side covering him with foul Cloaths, and he endeavouring to get out.[3]

This group is followed by:

Venus and Cupid
The Comic Muse in a Chariot drawn by 5 Satyrs . . .
All the Chorus (6 Boys and 20 Men dress'd in a Uni /
form like Arcadian Shepherds) Two and two
singing.

[1] Elizabeth P. Stein, op. cit., 110.
[2] Ibid, 86–8.   [3] Ibid, 110.

Chorus for the Pageant. by Bickerstaff.
Hence ye prophane! and only they, . . .
3 Graces / Apollo with his Lyre.
The Statue of Shakespeare supported by ye Passions /
    and Surrounded by the seven Muses with their /
    Trophies. (pp. 88–89.)

'The Kettle Drum drawn in a Carr/6 Trumpets' usher in groups from the following tragedies: *Richard III, Cymbeline, Hamlet, Othello, Romeo and Juliet, Henry V, King Lear, Henry VIII, Macbeth, Julius Caesar,* and *Antony and Cleopatra.* The stage directions for *Hamlet* are interesting:

Ghost with a Truncheon

Hamlet⎫
Queen ⎬in ye Closet Scene follow^g ye Ghost in horror

Ophelia mad with Straw etc.
2 Gravediggers. a Pick ax and Spade. (p. 89.)

In *Henry V* Fluellen with a leek 'makes Pistol eat ye Leek'. In *King Lear* Edgar appears 'in the mad dress with a Staff'. Thunder and lightning are indicated. Macbeth and Lady Macbeth are followed by 'Cauldron drawn by 4 Daemons, the Cauldron burning – Hecate and 3 Witches following the Cauldron'. Antony and Cleopatra have a retinue of 18 – 4 Persian guards, 10 blacks, and 4 eunuchs (pp. 90–91).

This is the last tragedy of the group. It is followed by –

Minerva – / Demon of Revenge with a burning Torch –
The Tragic Muse drawn in a Chariot by / 6 Furies – and
    attended by / Fame / Grief / Pity / Despair / Madness / 3
    Furies following the Chariot. Mars / 6 Soldiers with Swords
    and Shields / 9 Soldiers with Spears.

The Bells ring'em off and the Scene changes to / a Street in Stratford.
End of the first part. (p. 92.)

The Second Part is much briefer. Scene I shows the two country girls Nancy and Sukey, known for their duet 'The Country Girl' included in *Shakespeare's Garland*. The scene is obviously designed to make it possible to include more songs. Sukey is the more sophisticated of the two, for she has been to Birmingham and Coventry and tries to explain to Nancy who this Shakespeare they are celebrating is, by singing the ballad, very popular at Stratford, of 'Sweet Willy O'. Nancy, unsatisfied, answers with 'All this for a poet — o no'; they finish the duet and leave. The Irishman, who is drunk, hears them, runs after them but soon comes back. He asks a boy when the pageant will be coming, only to be told that it has long since passed and that everyone is now on their way to 'the round house on the meadow'. It is beginning to rain, and the Irishman, disconsolate, complains of the rain and the three hundred miles he has travelled to —

. . . lie in a Post-Chaise without Sleep, and to Sleep when I shou'd be awake, to get nothing to ate, and pay double for that — and now I must return back in the rain, as great a fool as those who hate to stay in their own Country, and return from their travels as much Improved as I myself shall when I go back to Kilkenny — However I'll try and get into some Corner of ye Round House too — and if I can't get in, Ara! I'll go home and be nowhere. (p. 97.)

The last scene follows. In the Huntington MS a memorandum in Garrick's own hand gives the following stage direction:

Last Scene

Is a magnificent transparent one — in which ᵗhe Capital Characters of Shakespeare are exhibited at full length — with Shakespeare's statue in ye Middle crown'd by Tragedy and Comedy,

M

fairies and Cupids surrounding him, and all the Banners waveing
at ye Upper End. Then Enter the Dancers. . . . (p. 100.)

The dancers are followed by the 'Tragic and Comic
troops' and the scene opens with the Chorus singing
'This is the day, a holiday! a holiday!' Then comes '*A
Dance of the Graces — Muses etc/After the Dance they all
come forward and Sing the following Roundelay.*'

> . . . . . .
> Sisters of the tuneful strain!
> Attend your Parents Jocund train,
> 'Tis fancy calls you, follow me
> To celebrate the Jubilee.

In nine stanzas they summon Shakespeare's characters both comic and tragic to come 'To celebrate our
Jubilee'. Mr Vernon sings the last stanza:

> But see in Crowds, the Gay, the fair,
> To the Splendid Scene repair,
> A Scene as fine, as fine can be,
> To Celebrate our Jubilee.

*Every Character tragic and Comic Join in the Chorus and go | back
during which the Guns fire, bells ring etc. etc. and the | Audience
applaud.*

> *Bravo Jubilee!*
> *Shakespeare for Ever!*
> *The End.* (pp. 101–3.)

The music for the pageant was composed by Dibdin
and the chief characters represented by the principal
performers in the theatre. Some of the actors and their
parts are mentioned in the newspapers:

Touchstone – Mr. King; Benedick – Mr. Garrick; Beatrice –
Miss Pope; Falstaff – Mr. Love; Portia – Mrs. Barry; Comic

Muse – Mrs. Abington; Richard III – Mr. Holland; Hamlet – Mr. Cautherley; Romeo – Mr. Brereton; Lear – Mr. Reddish; Antony – Mr. Aikin; Apollo – Mr. Veron; Tragic Muse – Mrs. Barry.[1]

The Jubilee had an overwhelming success and was performed more than ninety times to crowded houses during the season of 1769–70.

The reviewers agree that considered as spectacle and as entertainment *The Jubilee* is excellent and that the acting is good:

. . . this little piece, though it is intended entirely as a vehicle for exhibiting the Pageant, and performing the songs which were designed for the Stratford Jubilee, is, nevertheless, inconceivably pleasing in the representation. . . .[2]

. . . The Dialogue Part of this Entertainment is intended to give us as lively a Representation of what passed at the *Jubilee* of Shakespeare, as the Writer possibly could . . . Mr. King, in the Prologue, and in the character of the Country young Fellow, and Mr. Moody in the Irishman, perform so well, that they hide any defect that may be in the Dialogue. The general Hurry and Spirit of the Whole give us an agreeable Idea of the Distresses and Bustle of the *Jubilee* at Stratford, and the audience may enjoy both, without having the Inconveniences of partaking either of the one or of the other. . . .[3]

. . . If we consider this performance as a piece of writing, it has little or no merit, being destitute of fable, plot, and character; nor does it abound with wit and humour . . . But it may, nevertheless, escape criticism, as a necessary interlude to unite the different parts of a very agreeable and magnificent representation of the Jubilee, as it was originally designed, at Stratford.[4]

[1] *The London Chronicle*, Oct. 15–17, 26, 370.
[2] *The London Magazine*, Oct. 1769, 38, 397, 2.
[3] *The St James Chronicle*, Oct. 17, 1769, 4, col. 2.
[4] *The Town and Country Magazine*, Oct. 1769, 1, 550, 1.

Critics and spectators alike are unanimous in their praise of the procession in *The Jubilee*; some of their comments follow:

The pageant succeeds . . . This scene gave universal satisfaction, and must be allowed superior to that at Covent Garden.[1]

. . . splendid beyond conception.[2]

. . . the most magnificent Spectacle that ever was exhibited on any Theatre.[3]

The Procession of Shakespeare's Characters is the most superb that ever was exhibited, or I believe ever will . . . There never was an Entertainment produced that gave so much Pleasure to all Degrees, Boxes, Pit and Gallery.[4]

There are a few contemporary engravings of the Procession; the two copper-plates from *The Oxford Magazine*, which show characters from ten plays only, have been mentioned above (p. 126). More important is a large engraving, now at the Folger Shakespeare Library, entitled:

The principal characters in the procession of the Pageant exhibited in the Jubilee at Drury Lane Theatre. [London] Published according to Act of Parliament by J. Johnson and J. Payne, No. 72 St. Paul's Church Yard, Nov.ʳ 1ᵗ. 1770.[5]

It follows in every detail the description found in the Huntington MS, and it is so carefully done that it is

[1] *The Town and Country Magazine*, 1, 549, 2.
[2] *The London Magazine*, Oct. 1769, 38, 498, 1.
[3] Victor, op. cit., 3, 156–7.
[4] *Drury Lane Calendar*, ed. D. Macmillan, p. 143 quotes this from Hopkins, Diary, No. 4.
[5] The Reference Librarian informs me that it was found lying loose in a copy of J. P. Collier, *English Dramatic Poetry*, probably put there by the owner. It is not part of the book.

easy to read the names of the plays on the banners and to recognize the different characters in the groups (see illustration, pp. 154–5).

A German visitor to London during the 1769–70 season, Johann Wilhelm von Archenholz, was so impressed by *The Jubilee* that he went to see it twenty-eight times; he states that the performance took an hour and a half. He later wrote an enthusiastic account of it[1] in which he provides some quite important information about the staging of the procession and the properties used in it.

. . . The tragedies followed with their banners and heralds, and not only the most important characters in them but special suitable properties appeared with them. In *Macbeth* one saw the big witches' cauldron; in *Coriolanus*, this general's tent, ornamented with weapons, and in *Romeo and Juliet*, Juliet's tomb. When the characters approached the proscenium arch they acted out an important scene from their play in pantomime, whereby everything came wonderfully alive. King Lear showed his madness and Richard III his rage before the battle . . . Romeo took his poison and at that very moment Juliet awoke . . . Coriolanus's tent as well as Juliet's tomb were pushed by machines from the back of the stage to the front so very slowly that the action could be developed and finished without stopping the procession.

[Translated from the German.][2]

During the long run of *The Jubilee* minor changes were made in the Procession with regard to plays included, characters and scenes chosen and properties used. The lists of the pageant appearing in newspapers[2] after the

---

[1] Discussed by Martha W. England in 'Garrick's Stratford Jubilee: reactions in France and Germany', *Shakespeare Survey* (1956), 90–101.

[2] von Archenholz, *England und Italien*, Leipzig, 1787, 164–5.

[3] E.g. *The London Chronicle*, Oct. 14–17, 1769, **26**, 369–70.

opening performance and in the October issues of the Magazines[1] are identical and were probably given to reviewers by officials at Drury Lane. They contain groups from seventeen plays only, and it looks as if Garrick could not get groups from all nineteen plays ready in time for the opening. *Henry V* and *Two Gentlemen of Verona* are not included, but were probably added within a few weeks, for on October the 26th the newspapers announced that *The Jubilee* would be performed with additions. At this time the scene chosen for *Henry VIII* must also have been changed from Ann Boleyn's coronation to the scene with King Henry, Queen Katharine, and Cardinal Wolsey, which is shown on the engraving in the October issue of *The Oxford Magazine* (see p. 126).

Some very interesting information about the staging of the procession can be obtained from a small unpublished manuscript at the Folger Shakespeare Library, a list compiled by James Messink, the stage manager at Drury Lane, entitled *Order of the Pageant in the Jubilee*.[2]

obviously a plan for a revision of the pageant which was submitted to Garrick himself, as it contains brief notes addressed to him directly. In it *Henry VIII* is omitted and instead *Coriolanus* is included. As the German visitor quoted above (p. 167) mentions *Coriolanus* and not *Henry VIII* in his account, it must have been Messink's order of the Pageant that he witnessed, as the later list in the Huntington MS has *Henry VIII* but not *Coriolanus*, which must have been dropped

---

[1] E.g. *The London Magazine*, Oct. 1769, 38, 498, 1–2.

[2] James Messink [stage manager at Drury Lane Theatre], *Order of the Pageant in the Jubilee*. Unpublished MS, 7 pages. The Folger Shakespeare Library.

at a later date. It is worth noting that Colman had opened his 'Procession' in *Man and Wife* with *Coriolanus*.

As stage manager Messink carefully indicates in the margin of his lists the chariots and the pageants to be used by the different groups. They were large pieces of stage property, some on wheels drawn by costumed stage hands, others on platforms propelled by stage machinery or hidden stage hands. When Garrick had shown an interest in Moore's 'horseless carriages' (see p. 45) it is likely that he had hoped to use them, properly disguised, to propel the pageants through the streets of Stratford, where no stage machinery would be available, rather than for the transportation of his workmen from London to Stratford.

Messink describes the chariot, drawn by five satyrs, accompanied by '6 Loves with Large Antique masks', in which 'Comedey' sits (p. 3), and the chariot with a moon and stars, drawn by four Cupids in which the Fairy King and Queen ride (p. 2). It should be noted that Shakespeare's statue is not in a chariot but is carried by '4 Bacchanels – the Nine Muses with Tropheys Rang'd on each Side of the Statue' (p. 5). He marks only one 'pageant' for the comedy groups and that is for *The Tempest* which has 'a Ship in Distress'. A pageant with 'Mr. Nelson' and his large kettledrum leads the groups from the tragedies (p. 4). Other pageants indicated are: 'The Tent of Richard [III] Richard asleep/on the Couch' . . . (p. 4) 'Macbeth with 2 Daggers/Lady Macbeth – in hir mad Dress/*the Caldron*/4 Demons to Draw it' . . . (p. 5). The directions for the next three pageants have such interesting details that they will be quoted in full:

8 Romeo 4 Pageant	the Tomb – Juliet Lying in the Tombe, the Tomb ornemented with Escutchons Lamp &c. – Romeo standing on a Platforme Looking at Juliet befor it — a Gent — with a Banner Peter / Nurse / Fryar / Apothecary. (p. 5.) . . . . . .
11 Antony & Cleopatra 5th Pageant	Gent, (in Persian Dress) – with Banner 4 Persian Gards – Spears 4 Blacks / 2 Black boys – with Large Fans . . . . the boate that is in the Elopement[1] beautifully ornament^d; with Purpell sales etc. according to the Discripshon giveing by Mark Antony; in the Play – this S^r can be vary easey done, if you approove. (p. 6.)
12 Coriolanus 6 Pageant	8 matrons of Room Coriolanus'^{s}, mother, wife & Sone the Pageant to represent a kind of trone Compose^d of Tropheys of arms and Speers Tullus afegius Sitting on the Right hand of Coriolanus 6 Roman Soldiers at the Side where 　Coriolanus Sits; there Helmits, with horsetales 6 Volchon Soldiers – at the other Side where Tullus-afegius Sitting; with Plooms of feather in there Helmits when the matrons come down to the frunt the kneel, while the Pageant goes of, then folow, it melincoly. (pp. 6–7.)

[1] *The Elopement*, a pantomime by an anonymous author, performed the two previous seasons. See *Drury Lane Calender*, 240.

His description of the last 'pageant' with the Chariot of
the Tragic Muse does not differ from that of the later
Drury Lane MS (see p. 162). At the end of his list
Messink addresses Garrick directly as follows:

> worthey S͏ʳ I have kept the Pageants as
> far as posible, not to croude on one another
> but have sum smaller objects between
> Each Pageant, is to give time for the
> women to Dress for Corriolanus in the matrons
> Dresses   (p. 7.)

Messink's stage directions show very clearly how
elaborate and magnificent the production of *The Jubilee*
was and that great care had been taken with details. It
was a very costly undertaking which fully deserved its
long successful run.

Of course Garrick's enemies and rivals were green
with envy over *The Jubilee*'s overwhelming success at
Drury Lane and continued their attempts to ridicule him
and the Stratford Jubilee. In an anonymous 'Dialogue
between Mr. C— and Mr. F—'[1] the two men start
quarreling. Foote asks:

> But pray, Sir, how do you reconcile your own conduct to the
> rule of equity? – To forestal your own friend G — k, who
> had initiated you into all the arcana of the drama, was cer-
> tainly not acting the most grateful of parts.
>
> *Col.* Sir, the loss of Powell, and the necessity of bringing on
> something new, compelled me to the deed. (p. 525, I.)

Foote is annoyed with Colman's reference to 'his harmless satire' that is 'like fuller's earth' in his 'Prelude' to
Man and Wife; or, the Shakespeare Jubilee; the dialogue
continues:

[1] *The Town and Country Magazine*, Oct. 1769, I, 525–6.

Col. But why should you be so particularly angry at me? Have they not made more free with you, at Drury Lane? Have they not only ridiculed your speech, but personally taken you off?

F — te. As to Bannister's taking me off, it was so lame, so little like, and so ill placed, that scarce any one of the audience knew what he was about; and Moody's Kilkenny comparison, even if meant as an Irish bull, must be allowed pretty far fetched and nothing to the purpose.

Col. Whatever the success, the design was obviously to ridicule you and your speech. (p. 525, 2.)

Foote has no high opinion of Garrick's motives for celebrating Shakespeare:

Avarice and vanity prompted G — k to the deed. He wanted to fleece the people and transmit his name down to posterity, hand in hand, with Shakespeare. (p. 526, 1.)

Dibdin was known to hold a similar low opinion of Garrick and the motives that led him to plan the Stratford Jubilee in honour of Shakespeare. (See pp. 80–81.)

That Garrick was inordinately vain was a well-known fact always exploited by his enemies; that he had managed to build up a good-sized fortune as actor and manager by his ability as a shrewd and generally thrifty man of business, who often drove a hard bargain, was equally well known; but his deep genuine admiration for Shakespeare cannot be questioned, for while at Drury Lane (1747–76) he produced no less than twenty-seven of his plays.

When the Corporation of Stratford flattered him into giving a statue for the new town-hall by making him an Honorary Burgess, he immediately sensed the opportunity of coupling this event with a great festival in honour of Shakespeare, at which he would be the top figure. The Jubilee was his idea, and his alone, although he managed to get the support of the Corporation. His desire to make it a national celebration with entertainment provided not only for the fashionable world but also for the general public led him to conceive extravagant plans which included as attractions some features that had very little connexion with Shakespeare, such as the oratorio, the horse-race, the assemblies, and to a certain extent the masquerade; all these tended at times to overshadow the serious purpose of the festival. His attempt to please two very different types of visitors was not entirely successful and was the cause of some deplorable lapses in taste which called forth criticism from several sides.

The failure of the Stratford Jubilee was in a sense partly due to Garrick's gifts of showmanship which led him to create extensive advance publicity for the festival by such unorthodox means as the newspaper feuds, in which ironically enough he was assisted by his enemies. The interest aroused was such that the number of visitors at the Jubilee was twice as large as had been anticipated, with the inevitable result that many lacked proper accommodation and adequate catering and naturally complained both about prices and about lack of service. Add to this the unforeseen circumstance of the heavy rains that ruined so many of the planned entertainments, as no provisions had been made for such an eventuality. All this spelt failure, and to Garrick it was an expensive failure. The cost of producing the Stratford Jubilee was by some people estimated to be as high as £50,000, but Garrick would nevertheless have hoped that it might be a financial success. He had officially guaranteed that any profits from the Jubilee would be given to the town, whereas he would be personally responsible for any deficit that might occur. There was a sizeable deficit of about £2,000, which Garrick did pay back to the Corporation in instalments.

As Garrick's friend Joseph Cradock later intimated (see p. 68–69), it may have been a blessing in disguise that the procession was rained out at Stratford, for it was no doubt better suited to presentation on the stage, where the audience is at a certain distance, and full use can be made of lighting and make-up. In bright sunlight any imperfections in costumes and stage properties would be mercilessly exposed, and they might appear sleazy and tawdry; whereas, by means of transparencies and other special lighting on the stage, the illusion could be heightened and the proper mood created. The theatre audiences would also be more disciplined than a miscellaneous crowd lined up along the street, exposed to sun, rain, and wind, and shouting, pushing and shoving to get a good view of the procession.

By the great success of *The Jubilee* at Drury Lane, Garrick saw some of his ideas for the festival vindicated. He later admitted that his plans for the Stratford Jubilee had been extravagant and referred to it as 'my folly'. But the whole history of the Jubilee shows Garrick, his spirit unbroken, proving his flair for showmanship by transforming his folly at Stratford into his glory at Drury Lane.

Index

An Account of the Armed Corsican Chief, 97–98, 99, 100

Arne, Dr Thomas, musical composer, 11, 29, 33, 57; *Ode on Dedicating a Building*, etc., 11, 71, 79, 80, 82, 124, 125, 173; *Judith, an Oratorio*, 10, 29, 55–56, 57, 112, 132, 137, 138; Songs, Ballads, etc., 52, 60

Amphitheatre, the, or the Great Booth, Stratford, 12, 13, 14, 15, 28, 54, 59, 63, 66, 67, 69, 75, 95, 96, 102, 103, 104, 106, 109, 114, 132–3, 138, 145, 150–1

Angelo, Domenico, 16, 28, 45–46, 47, 65, 94, 95, 138

Angelo, Henry, 17, 28, 45–46, 68, 94, 96, 98

Archenholz, Johann Wilhelm von, 167

Assembly balls, 24, 25, 64, 104, 106, 112, 173

Avon, river, in flood, 75–76, 80, 96, 100, 102, 103

Aylward or Ailwood, Theodore, musical composer, 34, 52

Baddeley, Mrs Robert, singer, 55, 75–76, 125, 153

Baldwin, Richard, publisher, 94, 105

Bannister, Charles, actor, 153, 159, 172

Barthelemon, François Hyppolyte, musician and song-writer, 52, 55

Barthelemon, Mrs, singer, 22, 55

Barton, Margaret, 6

Becket, Thomas, bookseller, 35, 58

Bickerstaffe, Isaac, dramatist, 34, 48, 93, 128, 162

Birthplace, Shakespeare's, 2, 58, 59, 69

Boaden, James, editor, 6, 7, 8, 28, 30

Boswell, James, 18, 20, 21, 42, 48–50, 56–57, 62, 63, 64, 68, 77–78, 90, 97–98, 99, 105–6, 107, 110–11, 123, 126; as a Corsican Chief, 49, 57, 94, 95, 99, 100, 133; *Verses in the Character of a Corsican*, 94–95, 100, 105

Boyce, Dr William, musical composer, 30, 34

Burke, Edmund, 83

Cannon, 19, 51, 53, 65, 111, 158, 159

Capell, Edward, editor, 1, 41, 117

Carey, George Saville, author, 127, 143; *Shakespeare's Jubilee, A Masque*, 58, 127–30

Carlisle, Frederick Howard, fifth Earl of, 64, 91

Champness, Mr, singer, 55, 125, 153

Clandestine Marriage, The, by D. Garrick and G. Colman, 88, 144

Clopton family, the, 3

Colman, George, the Elder, dramatist, 48, 88, 97, 107, 117, 143, 144–52, 169, 171–2; *Man and Wife, or, The Shakespeare Jubilee*, 144–52, 169, 171

Cooke, William, biographer, 43

Country Girl, The, A Comic Serenata, 93, 94, 163

Covent Garden, The Theatre Royal, 143, 144, 145, 146, 150, 151

Cradock, Joseph, 14, 16, 31, 46, 55, 67, 68, 81, 89, 102, 144, 174

Davies, Thomas, bookseller, 36, 89, 101

Dibdin, Charles, dramatist, and song-writer, 34–35, 51–52, 55–56, 60, 61, 62, 75, 80–81, 93, 100, 128, 153, 164, 173

Dorset, John Frederick Sackville, third Duke of, 12

Drury Lane Calendar, 1747–1776, 124, 166

Drury Lane, The Theatre Royal, 1, 17, 27, 35, 51, 55, 81, 114, 123–5, 143, 144, 145, 146, 153, 154, 166, 174

Dryden, John, 1, 37, 117

England, Mrs Martha W., 64, 83, 92, 167

Fireworks, 10, 16–18, 47, 65, 94, 95, 106, 110, 112, 113, 115, 138

Fitzgerald, Percy H., biographer, 101

Foote, Samuel, comedian and dramatist, 36, 42, 48, 69, 78, 97, 101, 109, 114, 115, 132, 137, 140, 148, 171–2; 'The Devil upon Two Sticks', 113, 114, 115;

'Devil's Definition', 113, 141, 147, 159

Gainsborough, Thomas, 10

Garrick, Mrs Eva-Marie, 5, 10, 22, 64, 67, 100, 105, 106

Garrick, George, 13, 105

Garrick's Vagary: or, England run Mad, 135–9

Gastrell, the Rev. Francis, 3–4

Gentleman, Francis, author, 140, 148

Gray, Thomas, 29, 31, 117

Great Booth, the, see Amphitheatre

Great Collegiate Church, the, 22, 55, 56, 57, 132, 137

Grosvenor, Richard, first Earl of, 54, 59, 78, 98, 100, 104

Hall, Elizabeth (Lady Barnard), 3

Hall, Mrs Susannah (Shakespeare), 3

Halley's comet, 66

Havard, William, actor and poet, 30

Haymarket, Little Theatre, 42, 113, 114, 115, 140, 143

Horse Race, 25–27, 103, 104, 110, 113

Hunt, William, Town Clerk of Stratford, 8, 46, 53

Jackson, Mr, habitmaker and costumer, 35, 47, 96

Johnson, Dr Samuel, 1, 4, 21, 36, 37, 41, 48, 83, 105, 135, 145

Jonson, Ben, 1, 117, 140

Jubilee, The, by Garrick, 114, 146, 150, 152, 153–71

Judith, An Oratorio, see Arne, Dr Thomas

Keate, George, author, 7, 10, 37, 41

Kemble, John Philip, actor-manager, 22, 153, 156
Kenrick, William, author, 36, 40–42, 98, 118, 121–3
King, Thomas, actor, 63, 88–91, 94, 124, 148–9, 156, 158, 164, 165
Knight, Joseph, biographer, 11, 30

Lacy, James, co-manager of the Drury Lane Theatre, 12, 68, 107
Langley, Hugh, 33, 55

Macmillan, Dougald, editor, 124
Man and Wife, or The Shakespeare Jubilee, see Colman, George
Mann, Isabel R., 12
Masquerade, the, 24, 25, 35, 66, 94, 95, 96, 102, 105, 110, 112, 113, 133, 138, 143, 145, 146, 148, 150, 151, 173
Meacham, John, Mayor of Stratford, 53
Messink, James, stage manager at Drury Lane, 168–71
Milton, John, 72, 82, 117
Montagu, George, 24, 40
Moody, John, actor, 158, 165, 172
Moore, Mr, inventor of the 'horseless carriage', 44, 45, 115, 169
Morning Address, The ('Let Beauty', etc.), 35, 51, 158
Mulberry Tree, Shakespeare's, 3, 4, 5, 7, 8, 25, 39, 53, 139; relics carved from the wood of: mulberry box, 6, 8, 9, 10, 123; loving cups, 60, 62–63, 160; medal and wand, 53, 71, 92, 159; others, 5, 10, 25
Mulberry Tree, The, a ballad, 34, 60, 61, 62, 63, 132, 160
Murphy, Arthur, dramatist, 97, 101

New Place, Stratford, 2–4

Ode on Dedicating a Building, etc., 11, 29, 30–1, 58, 66, 67; presentation at Stratford, 69–77, 87, 103, 116, 126, 138, 159; comments on performance, 77–81, 110, 147–8; criticism of ode, 108, 113, 115, 118–23, 133, 139; publication of ode, 58, 115, 116–18; presentation at Drury Lane, 123–4, 157
Ode . . . to Le Stue, 123
Ogleby, Lord, character in *The Clandestine Marriage*, 88, 98, 102
Oman, Mrs Carola, 53, 88
Oration in Honour of Shakespeare, An (the 'prose eulogy'), 31–33, 82–87, 90, 92
Oratorio, *see* Arne, Dr Thomas
Order of the Pageant in the Jubilee, by Messink (MS.), 168–71

Pageant, the (or procession), 27–28, 66, 67, 68, 69, 103, 104, 110, 113, 126–7, 138, 143, 145, 146, 148, 150, 151, 152, 153, 158, 160–2, 165, 166, 167–71
Pembroke, Henry Herbert, tenth Earl of, 6
Peyton, John, host of the White Lion Inn, 14, 16, 35, 43, 46, 107
Pope, Alexander, 1, 83, 92, 117, 134
Pottle, Frederick A., 121
Powell, William, actor, 28, 145, 171

Queen Mab, A Cantata, by Dibdin and Bickerstaffe, 93, 128

Rains, heavy, 66, 68, 94, 95, 102, 110, 157

Reynolds, Sir Joshua, 18, 145
Road to Stratford, 19–20, 43, 131–2
Ross, David, actor-manager, Edinburgh, 63, 94
Ross, Mrs (the actress Fanny Murray), 63, 94
Royal Academy, 17–18

Scrub's Trip to the Jubilee, 140–1
Shakespeare's Garland, A Collection of New Songs, etc., 52, 57, 58, 61, 69, 93, 94, 116, 163
Shakespeare's Jubilee, A Masque, see Carey Sharp, Thomas, woodcarver of Stratford, 5, 21
Sisters of the Tuneful Strain, A Roundelay, 93, 164
Smith, William ('Gentleman'), actor, 27
Statue of Shakespeare (by Scheemaker), 5, 6, 7, 13, 69, 71, 76, 77, 78, 82, 129, 162, 169; crowning of, 27, 29, 79, 113, 124, 129, 150, 157, 158, 163
Steevens, George, editor, 5, 36, 37, 89, 117
Stein, Elizabeth P., 67, 156–64
Stratford Jubilee, The, A New Comedy, 140–1
Sweet Willy-O, a ballad, 60, 62, 163

Tait, Hugh, 10
Thompson, Capt. Edward, 100, 130, 134; Trinculo's Trip to the Jubilee, 130–5
Three Plays by David Garrick (ed. E. P. Stein), 67, 156
Town Hall, Stratford, 5, 7, 10, 11, 18, 53, 54, 66, 102, 106, 132–3

Transparencies, 17–19, 63, 65, 145, 162
Trinculo's Trip to the Jubilee, see Thompson

Vernon, Mr, singer, 55, 125, 153, 164, 165
Verses in the Character of a Corsican, see Boswell
Victor, Benjamin, theatre historian, 5, 19, 53, 59, 63, 66, 69, 71, 87–88, 92–93, 96, 103, 106, 132, 146, 166
Voltaire, François Arouet, M. de, 10, 89, 117

Walpole, Horace, 24, 40, 117
Warburton, William, author, 1, 36, 37, 117
Ward, John, actor-manager, 22
Warwickshire, a ballad, 34, 52, 60, 149, 159
Wheler, Francis, 5, 6
Wheler, Robert Bell, 3, 4, 5, 20, 21, 27, 43, 53, 54, 55, 58, 65, 71, 78, 79, 82–87
White Lion Inn, Stratford, 14, 15, 35, 50, 105, 109, 132, 159
Wilson, Benjamin, painter, 6, 11, 45; 'Shakespeare in his Study', 11
Witches, the Three, 98, 102; Mrs Bouverie 98, 102; Mrs Crewe, 98, 102; Mrs Payne, 102; Lady Pembroke, 98

Yates, Richard, actor, 98
Yates, Mrs Richard, actress, 28, 98